Editorial Comment:

There are times when pictures are just what looks like fun to look through.

Book:
PICTORIAL VIEW – Midwest Northwest, Illinois

Carol Lee Brunk
Designer, Photographer, Writer
Independent Educator Contractor
Self-Publisher
www.sightwordsataglance.com
Published in the United States

Copyright 2015

CONTENTS

PHOTOS
OF
CAT OFIEE

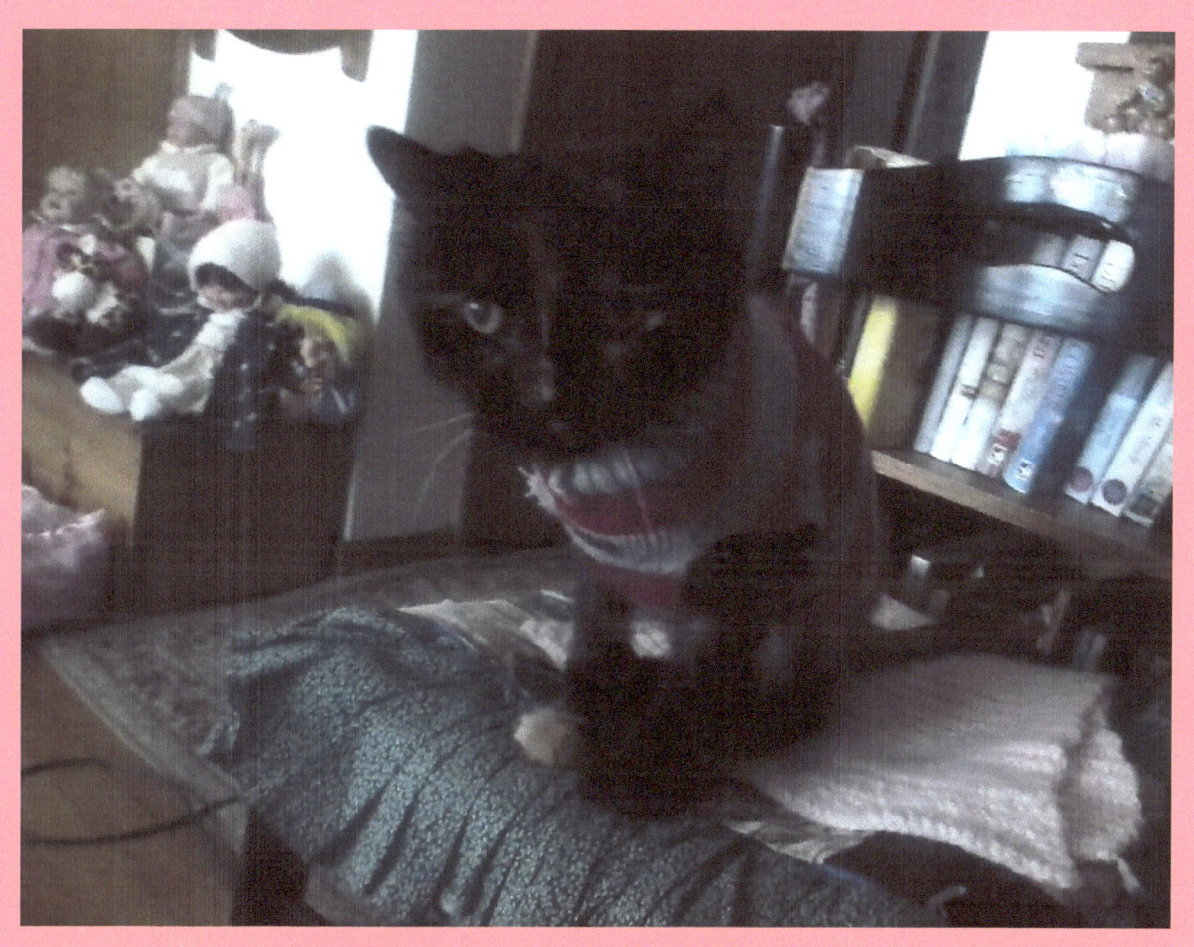

Dedicated to "Ofiee"

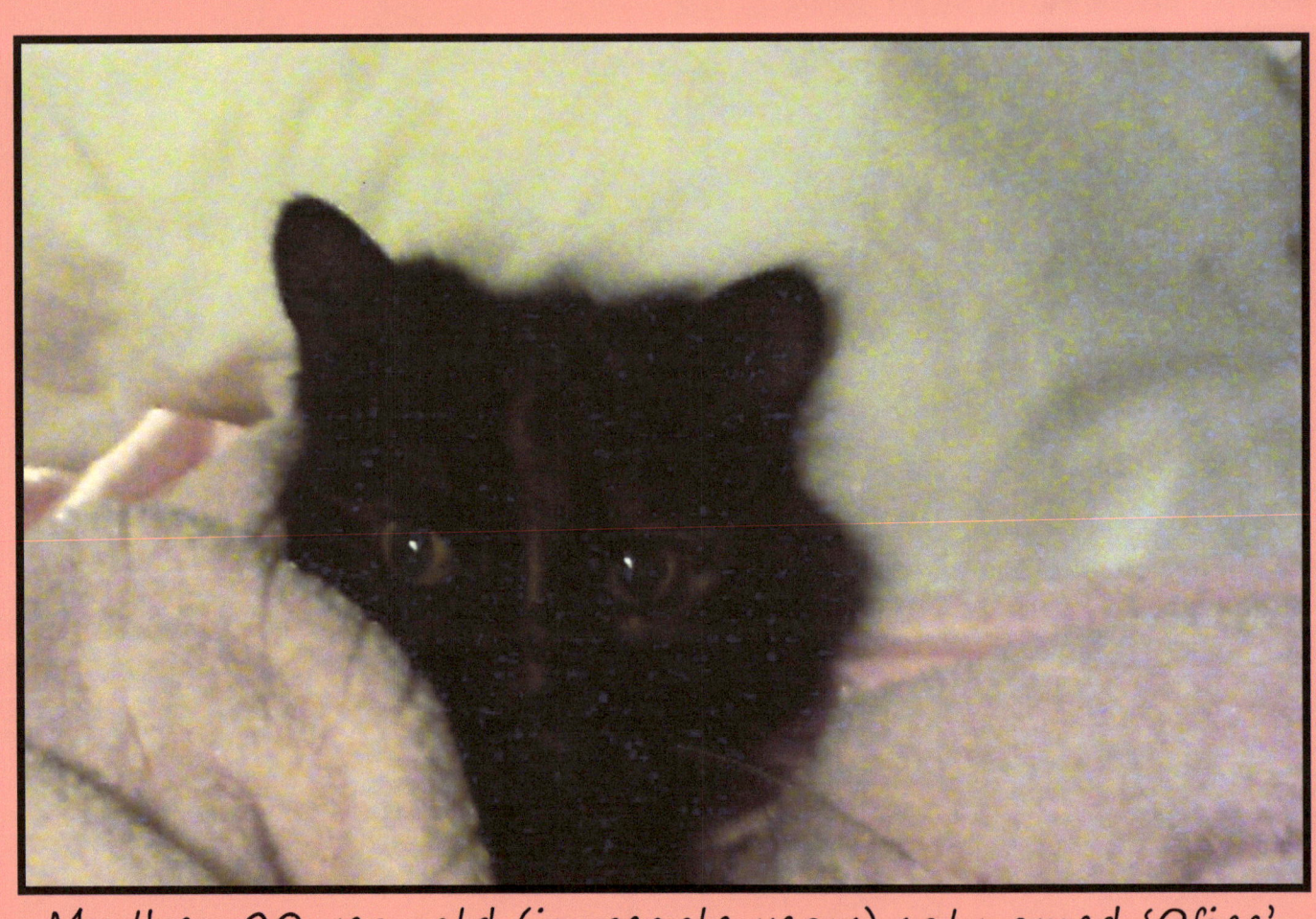

My then 20 year old (in people years) cat named 'Ofiee'

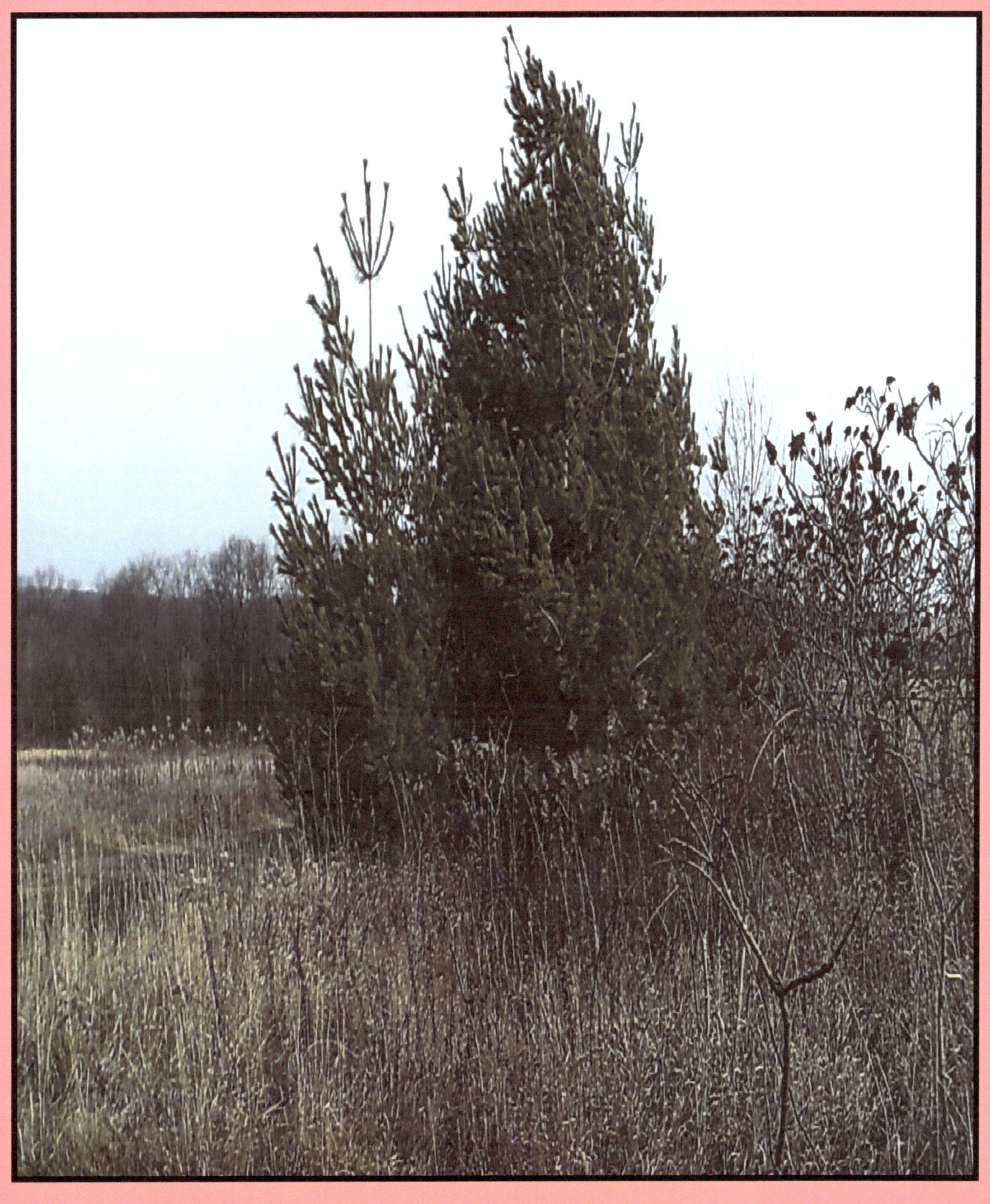

...Off the road trail outside OREGON, ILLINOIS... a walk, a drive for a pictorial view...

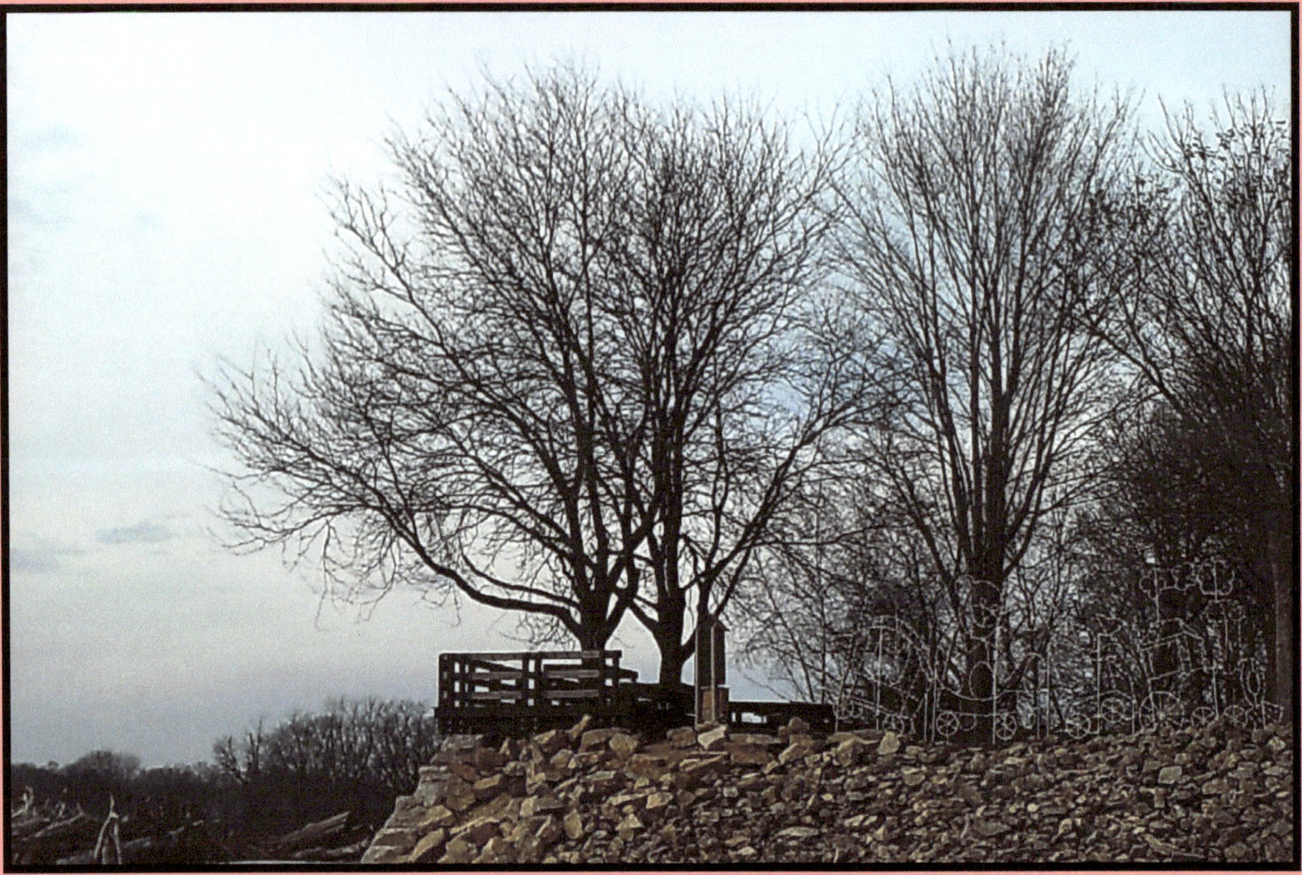

Quiet, peaceful, listen to the water flow...
Outside across the river from HANOVER SQUARE Mall from OREGON, ILLINOIS

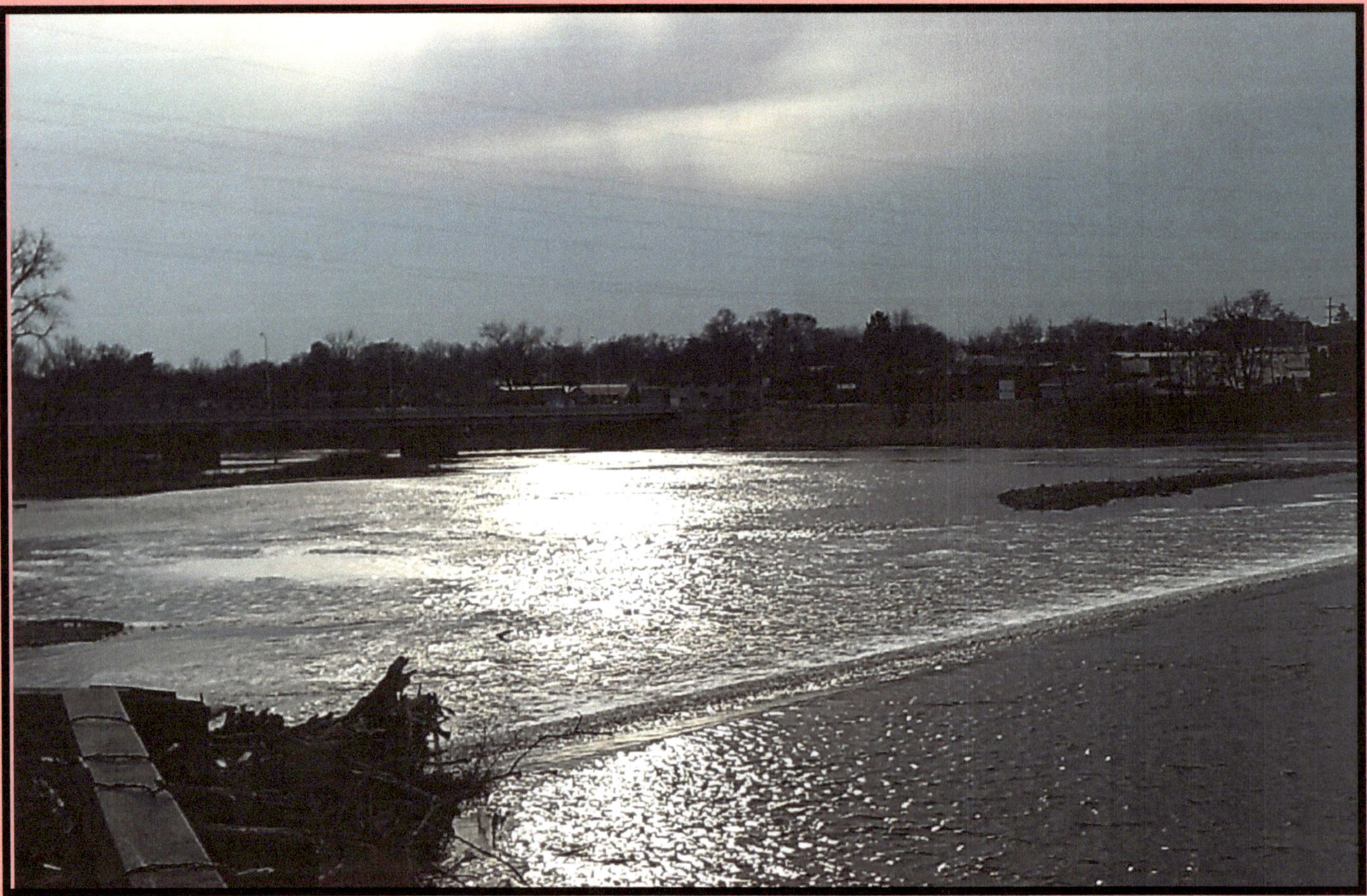

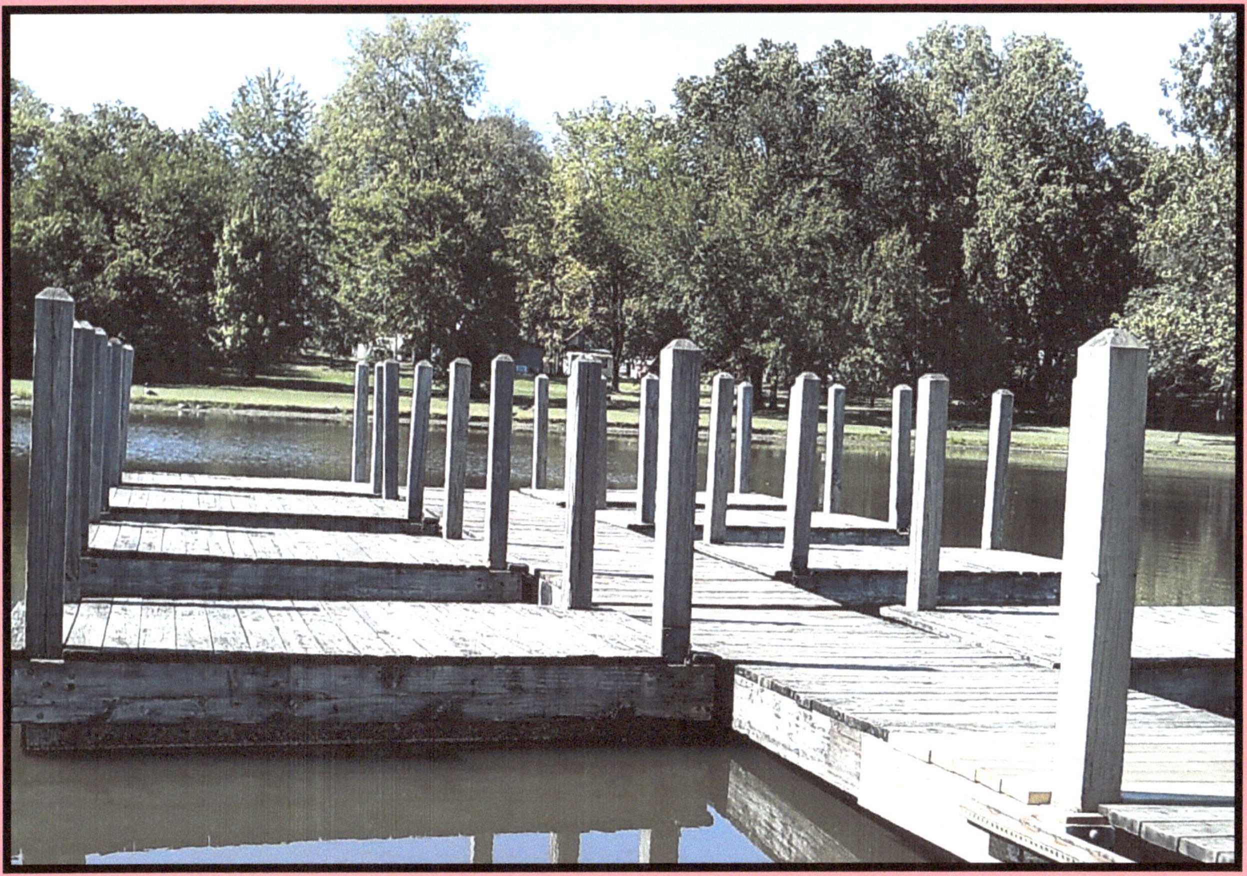

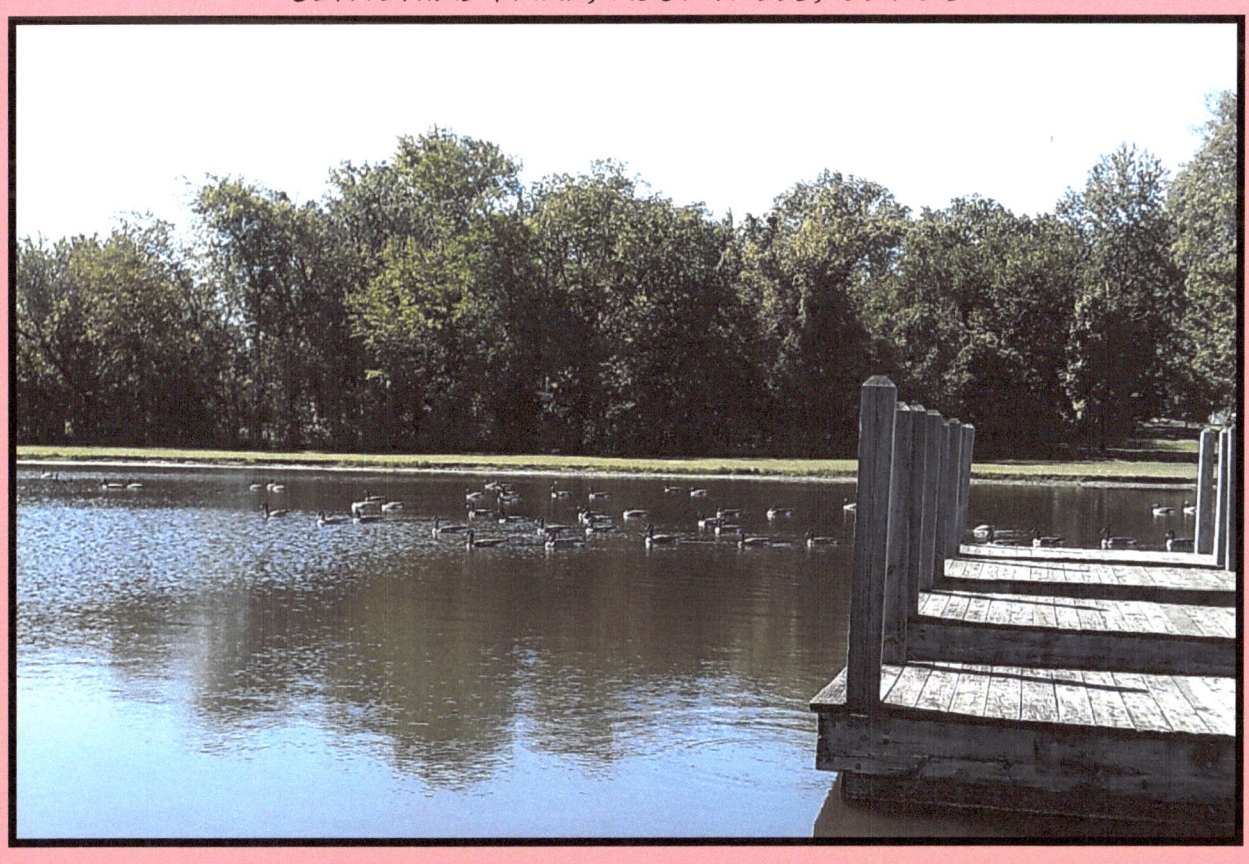

I was on a day for a feather parade to boat by...
CENTENIAL PARK, ROCK FALLS, ILLINOIS

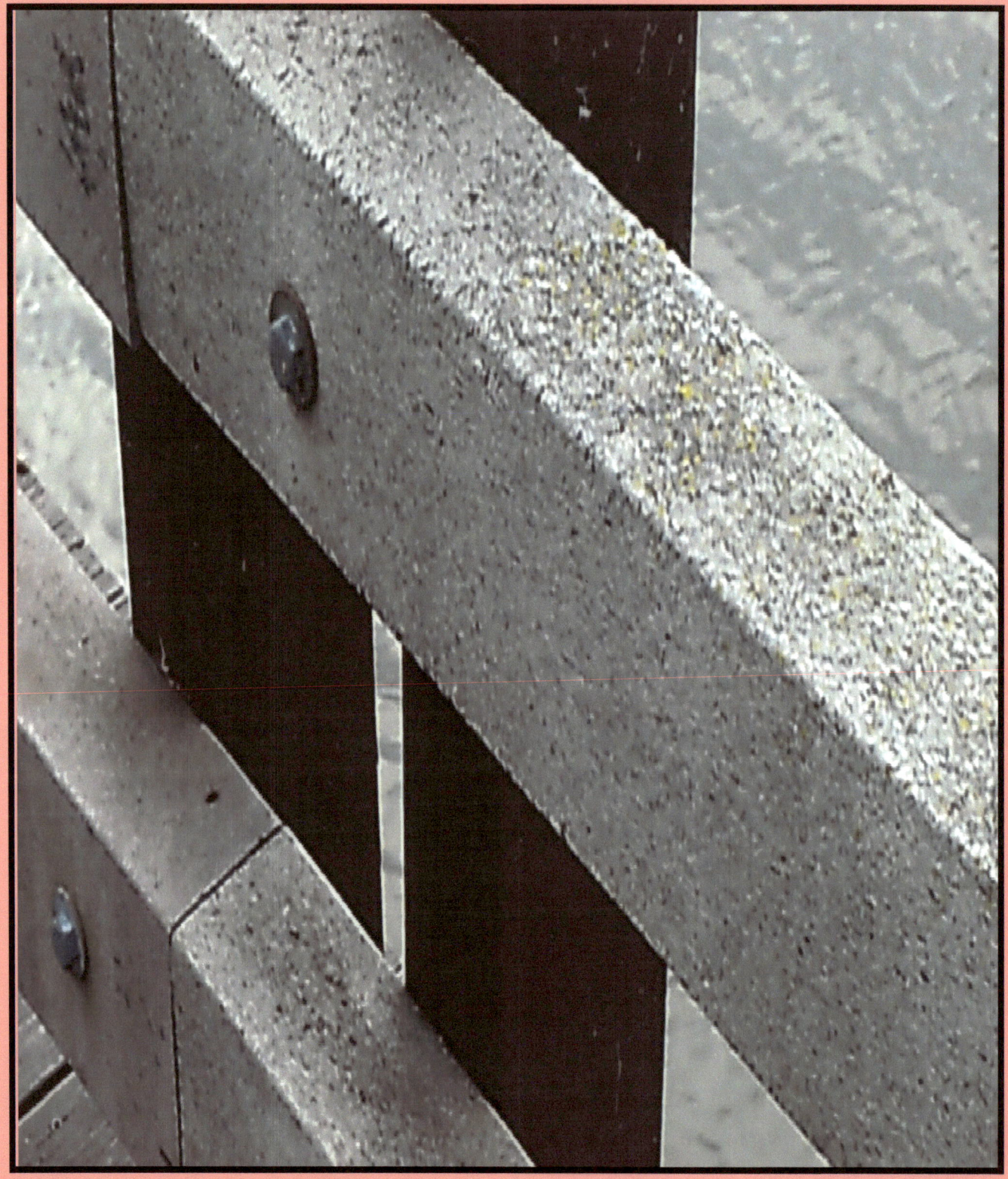

...The granite had a nice texture...Outside across the river from HANOVER SQUARE Mall from OREGON, ILLINOIS

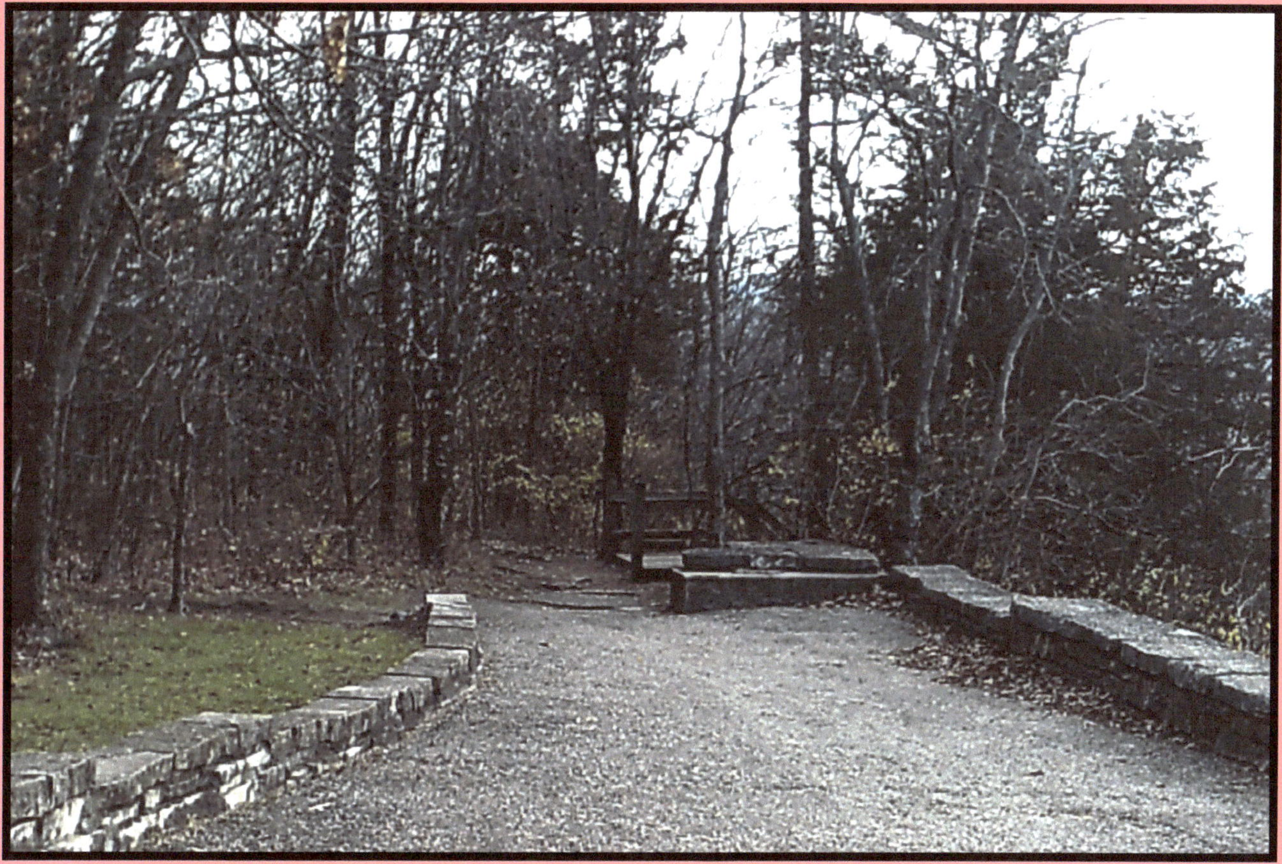

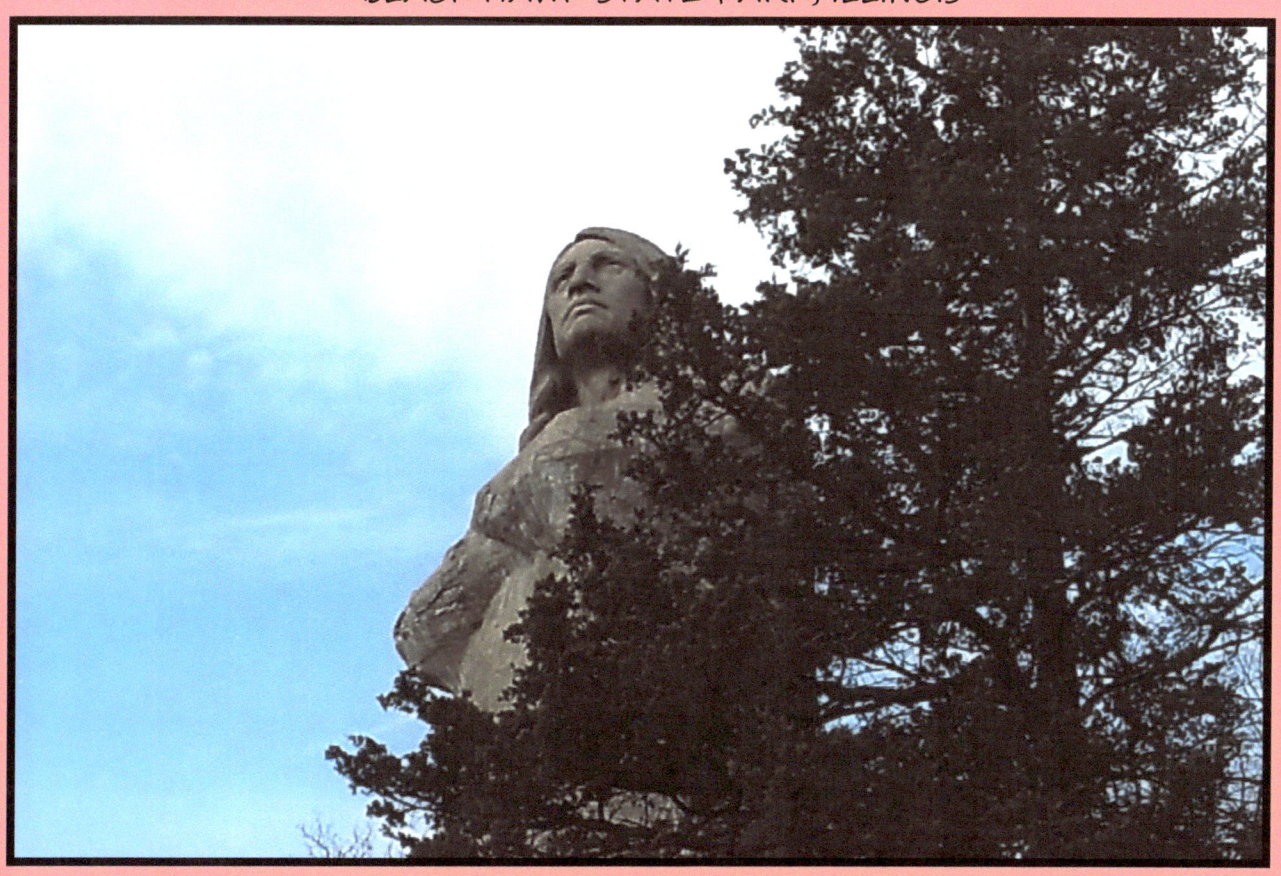

Autumn hike...look what was peeking at me...at the
BLACK HAWK STATE PARK, ILLINOIS

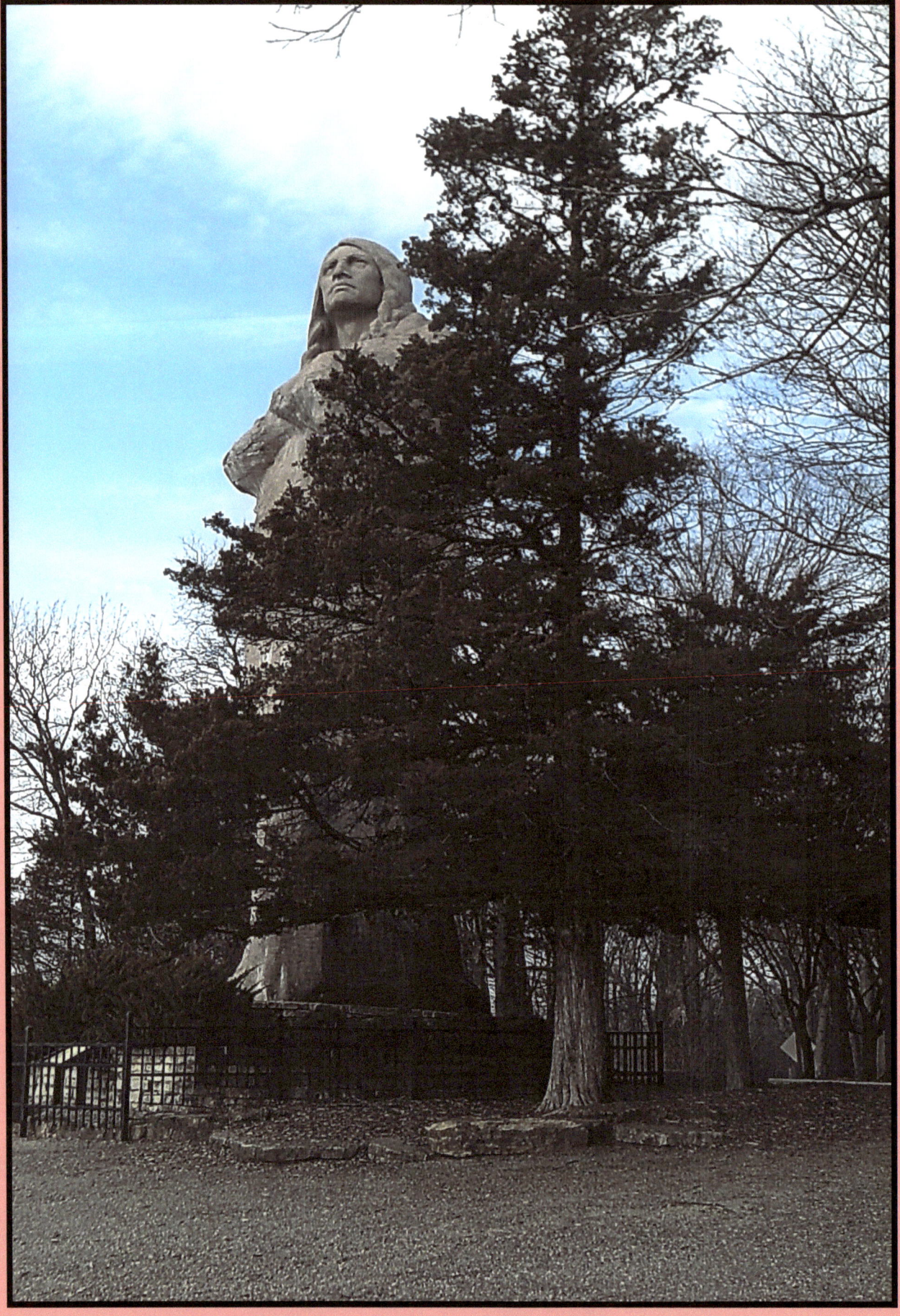

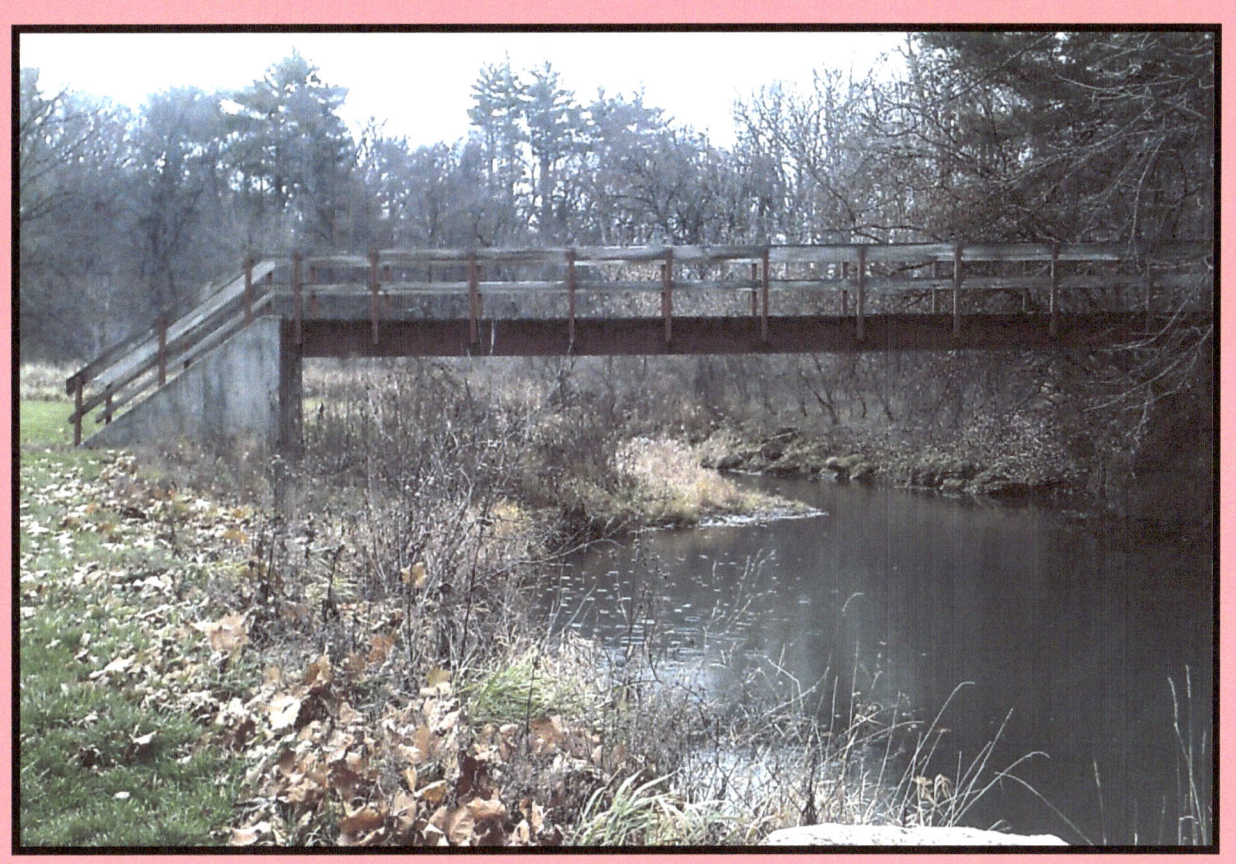

..not really waiting... but it was a nice walk...
WHITE PINES STATE PARK, ILLINOIS

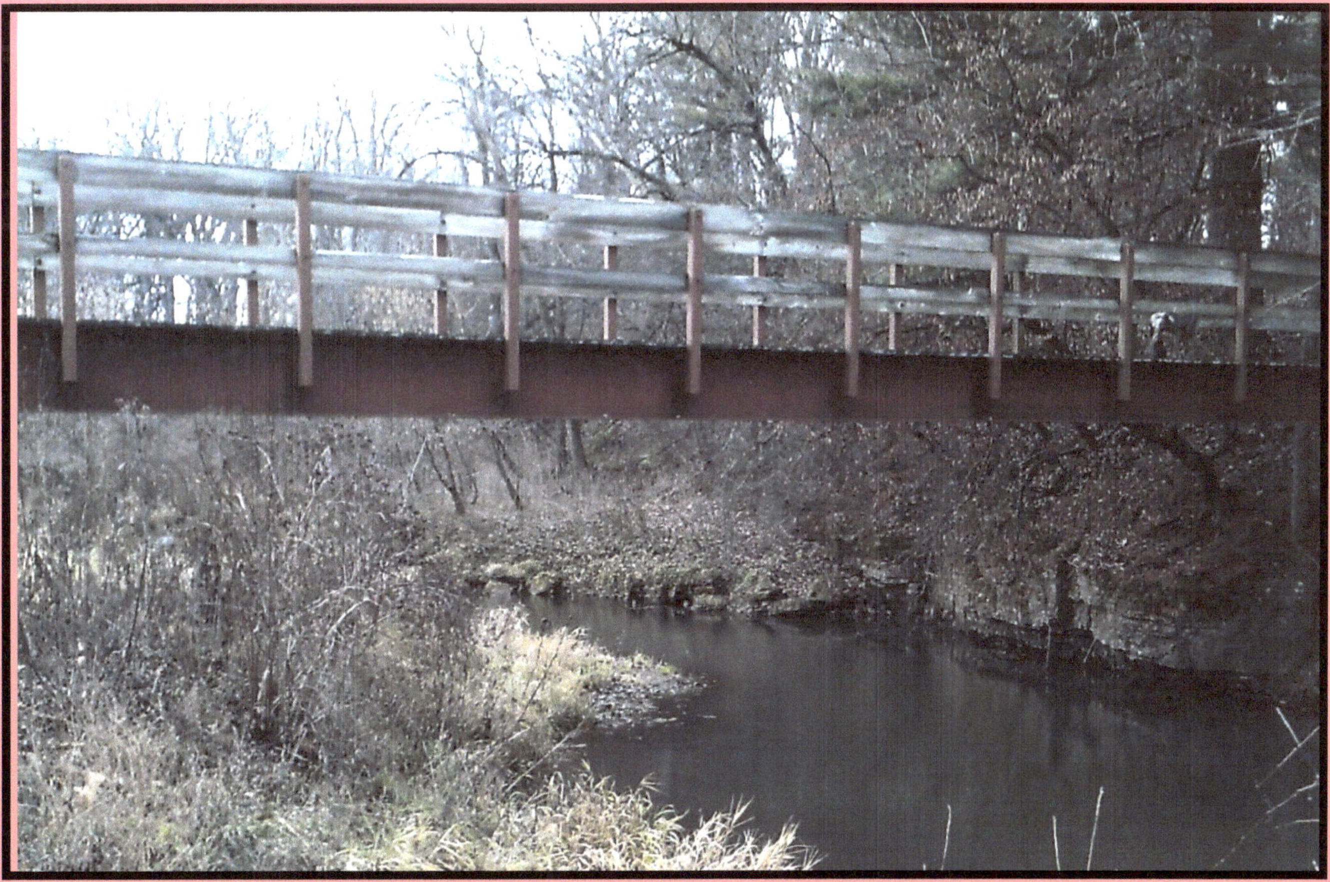

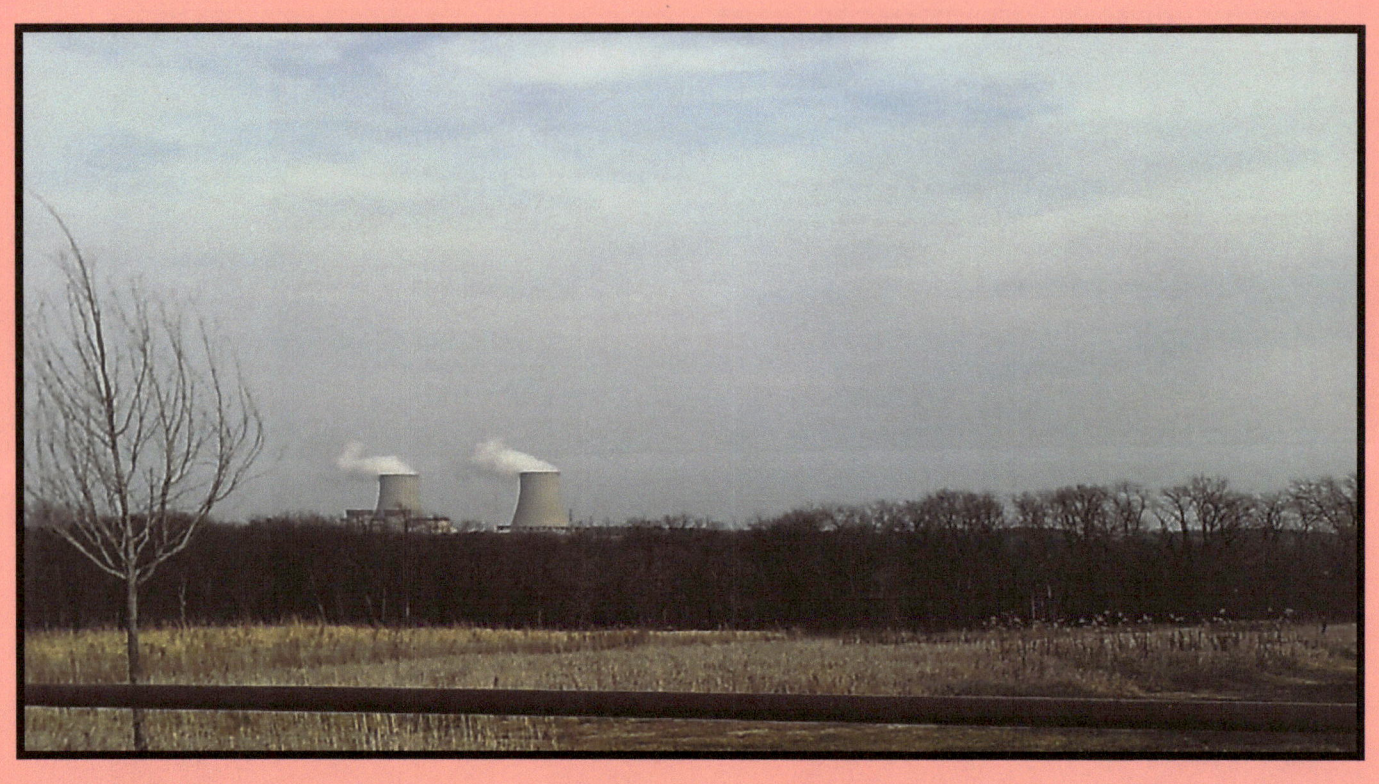

Smokey the bear had a difference of opinion of what smoked...a new reserve may become old ...BYRON, ILLINOIS

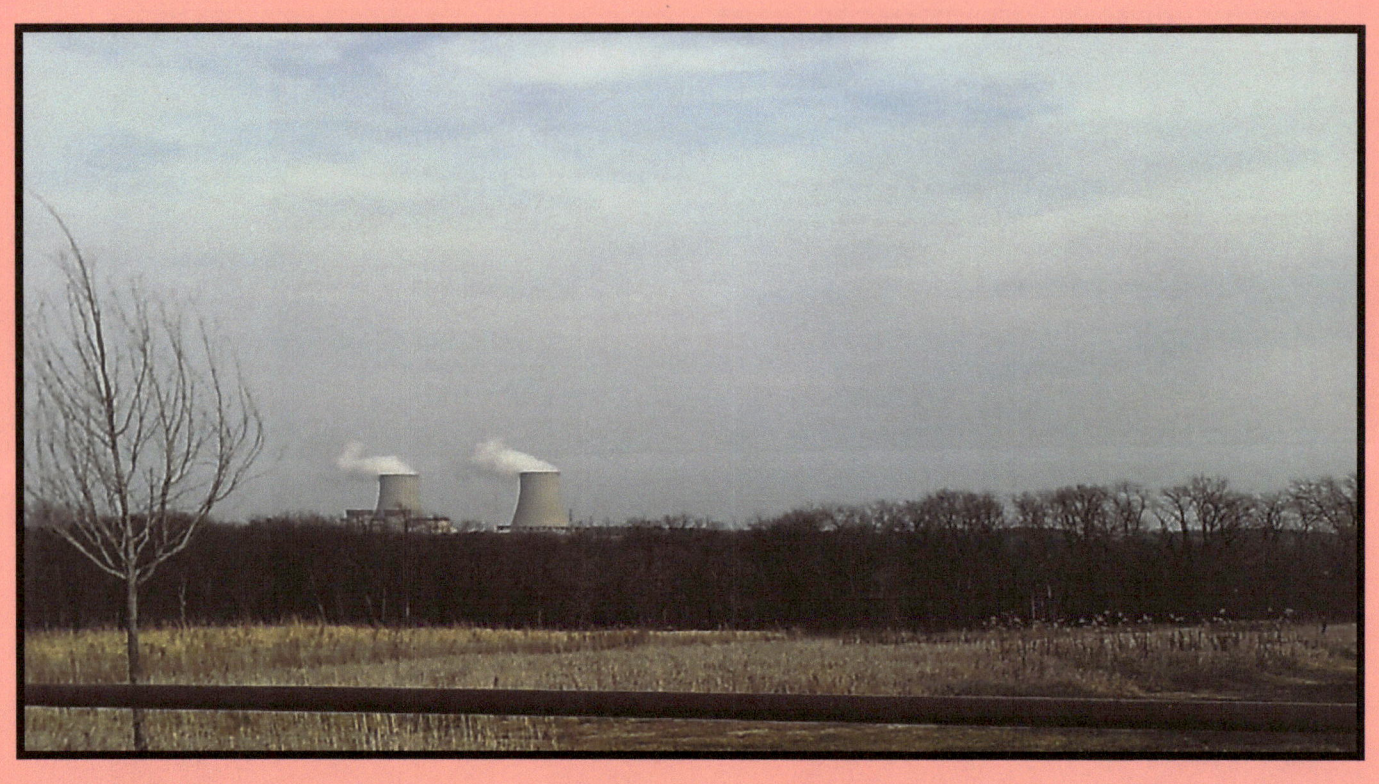

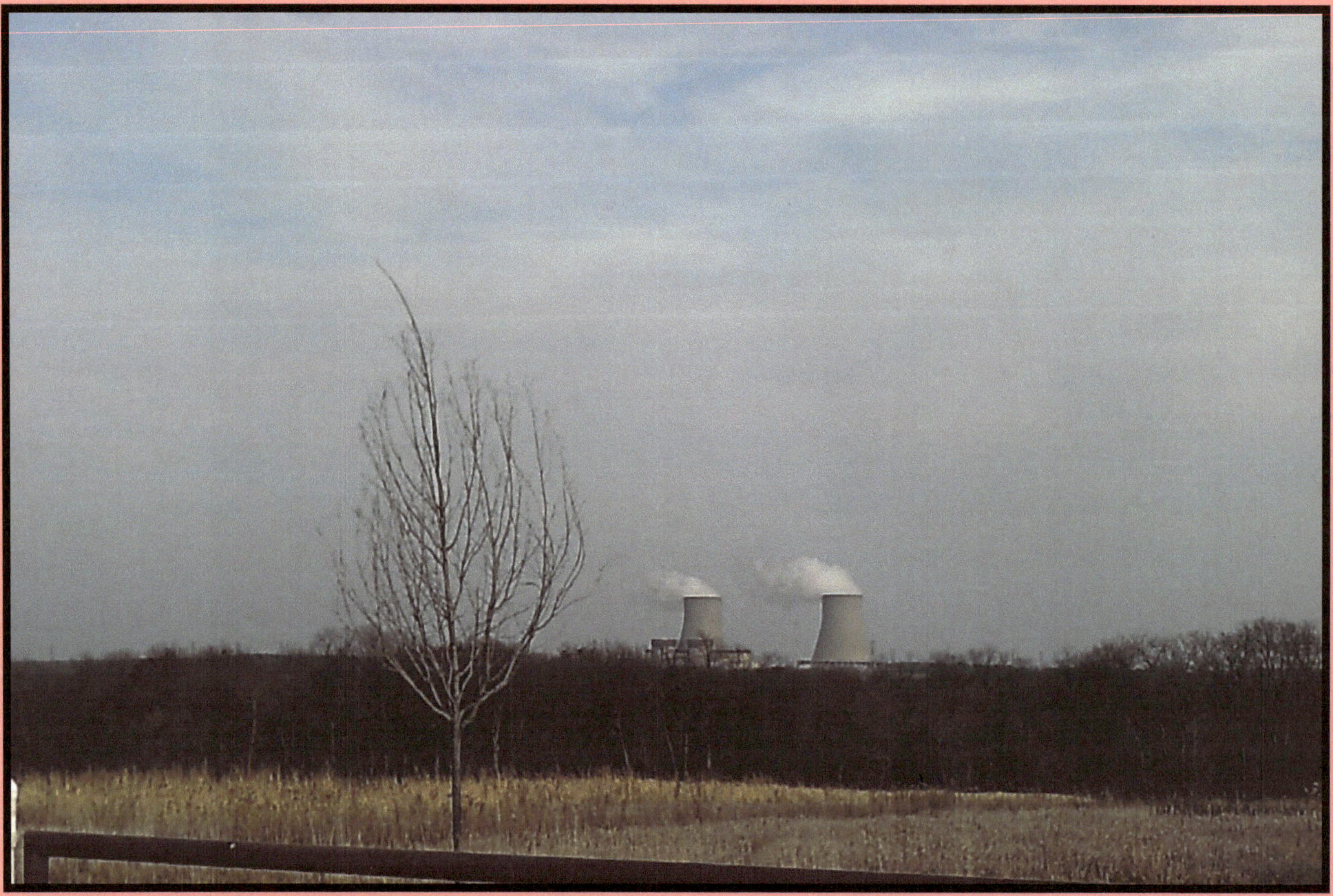

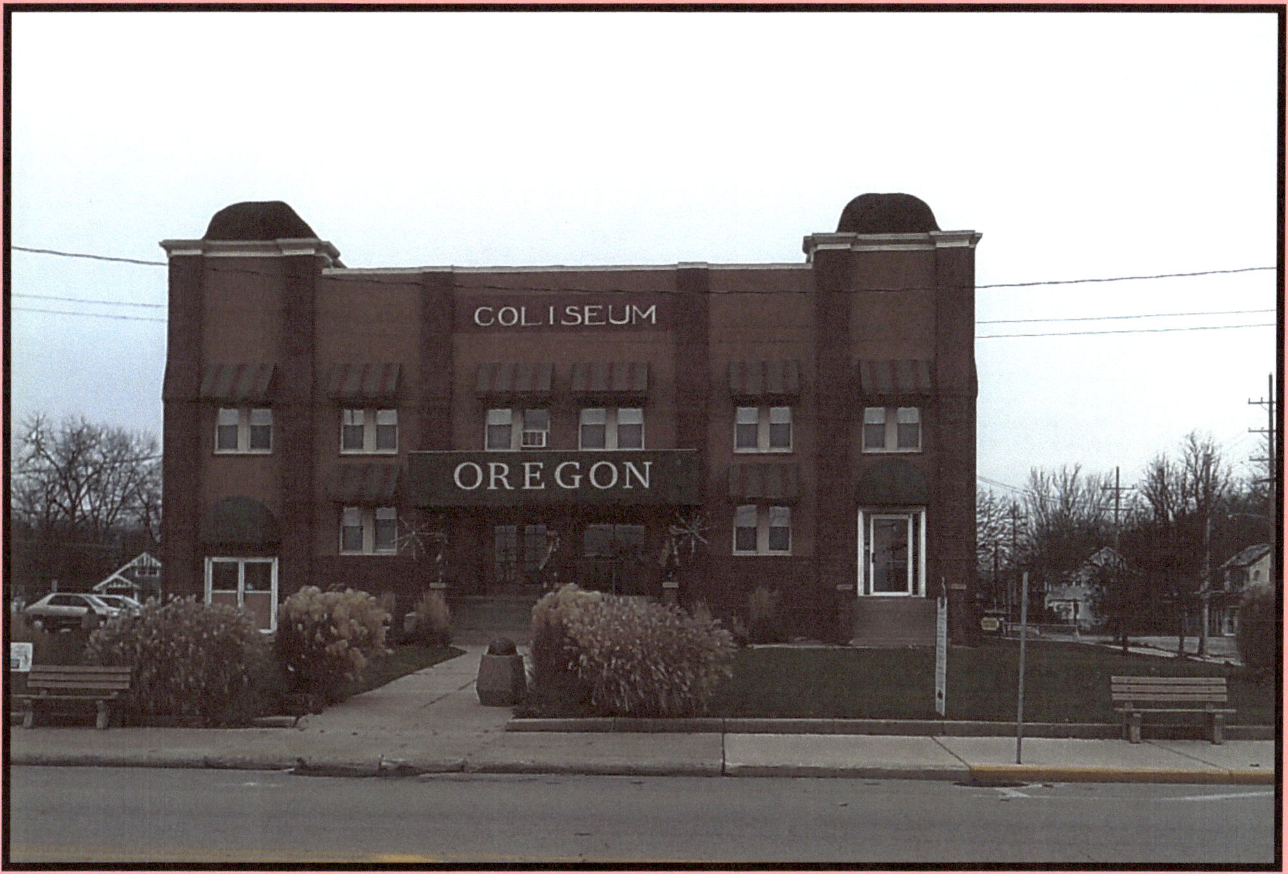

The coco is in the small building.. a .small town decorated for the upcoming holiday festival...OREGON, ILLINOIS

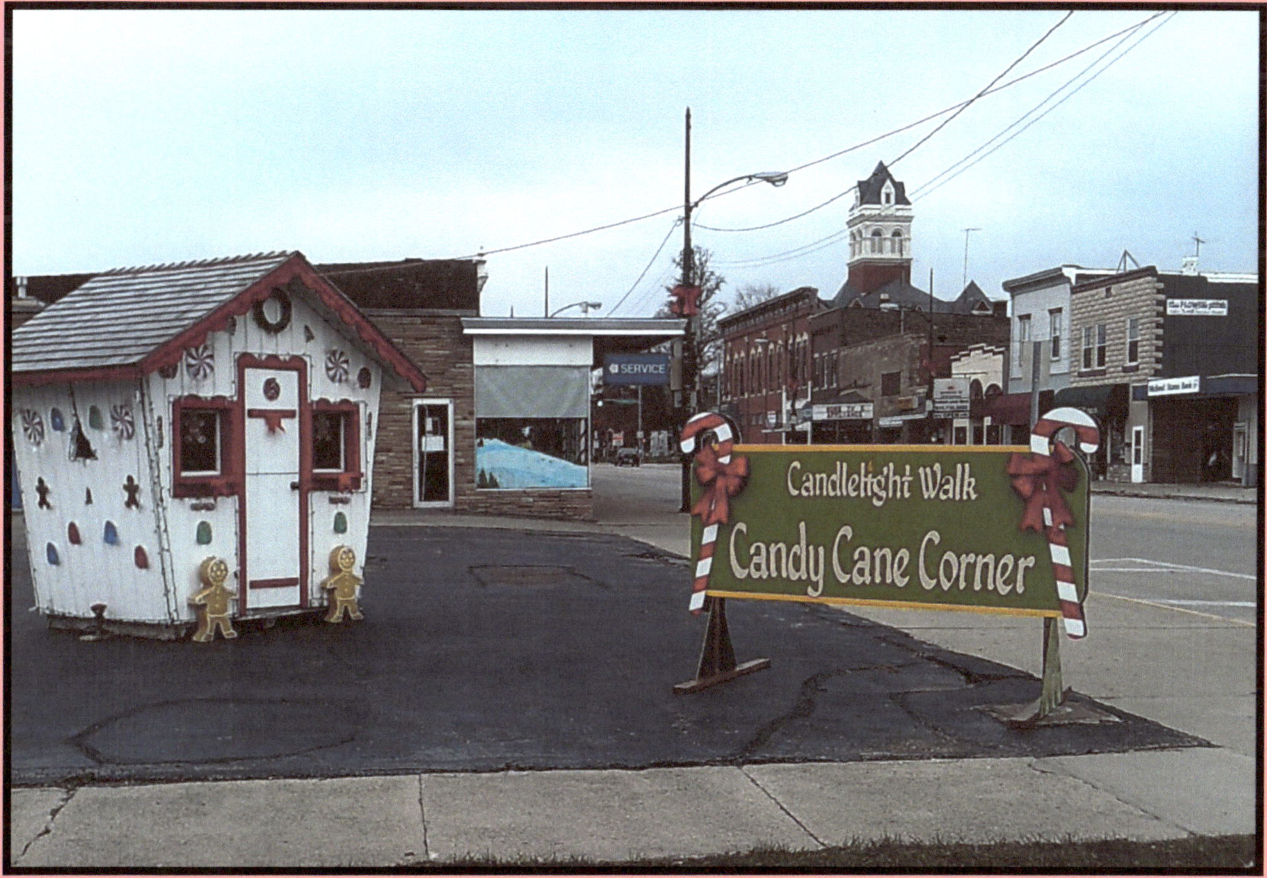

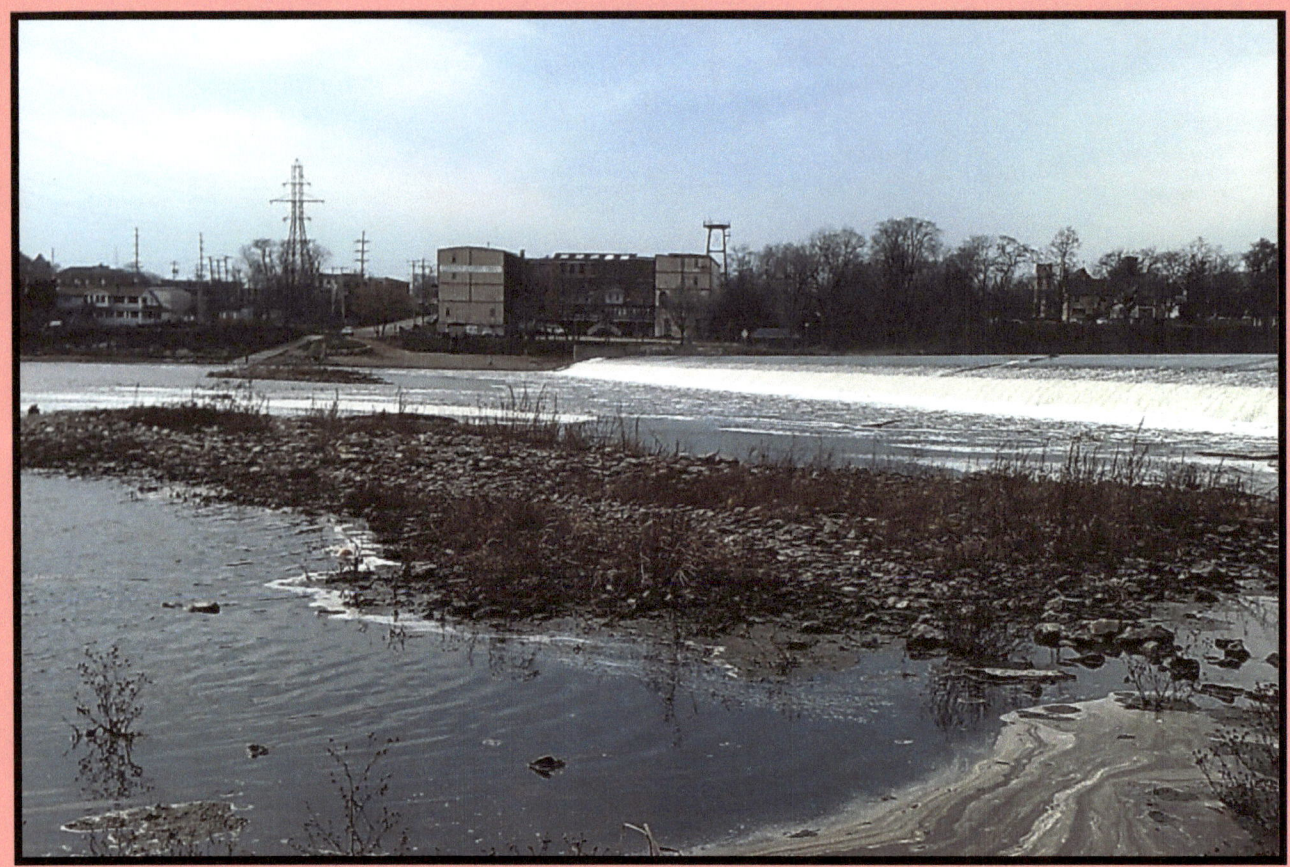

Quiet out there...outside across the river from HANOVER SQUARE Mall from
OREGON, ILLIOIS

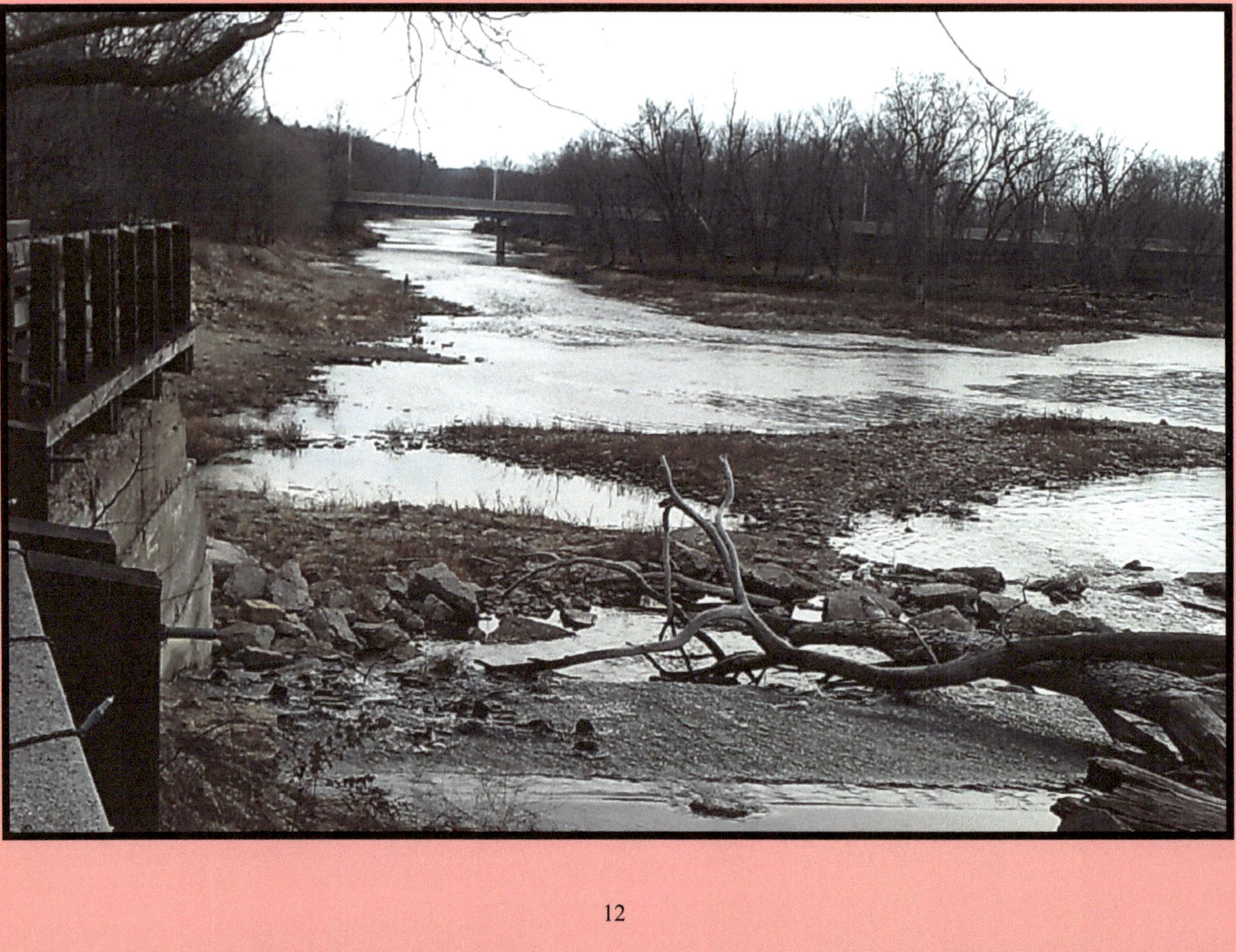

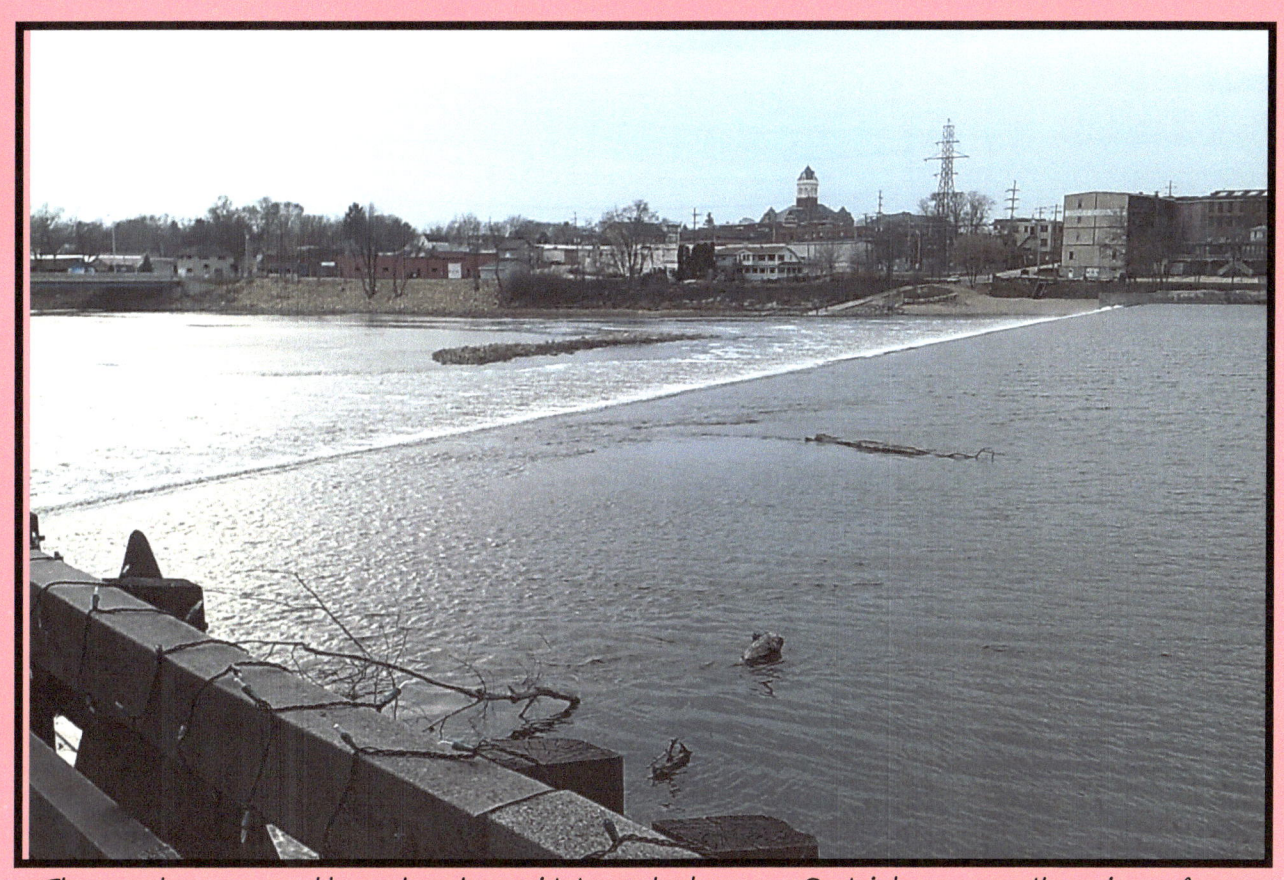

The rush was really a hush as it traveled over...Outside across the river from HANOVER SQUARE Mall from OREGON, ILLINOIS

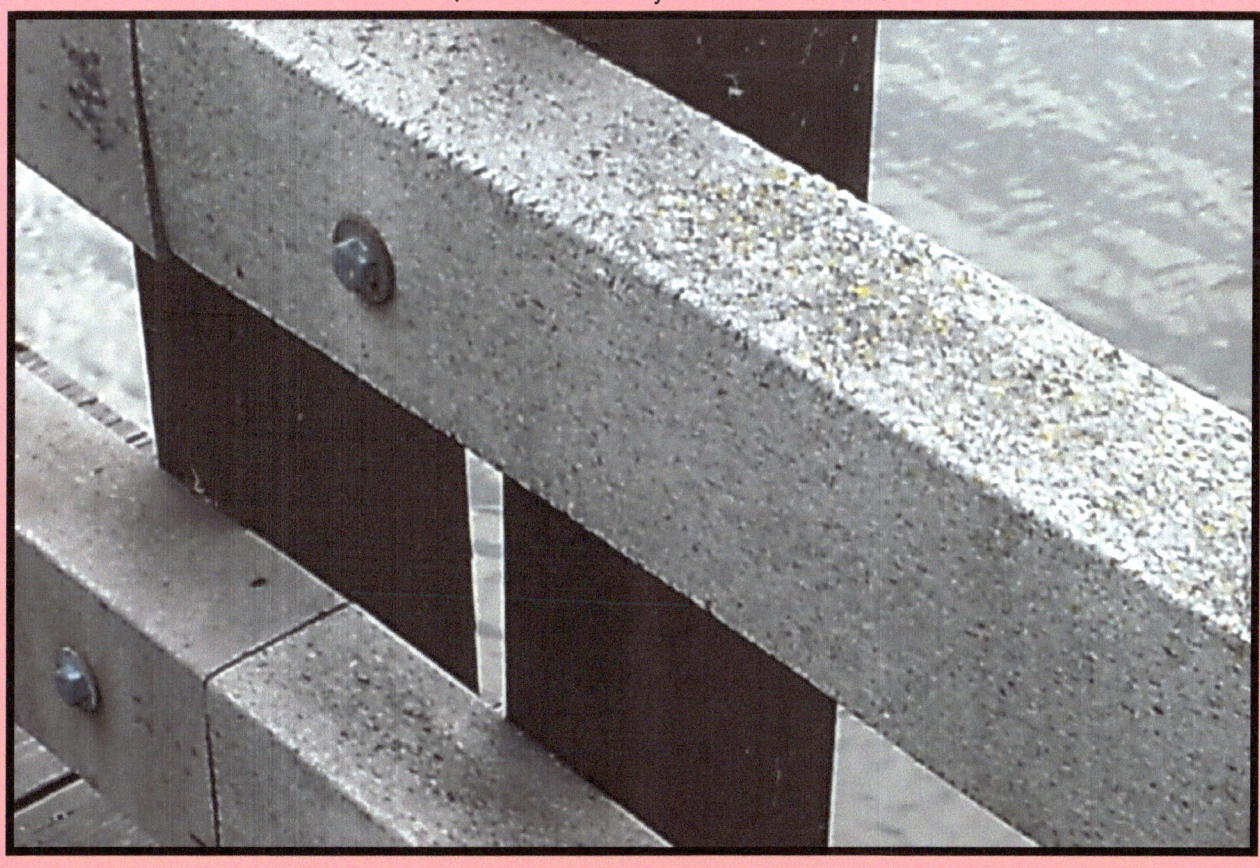

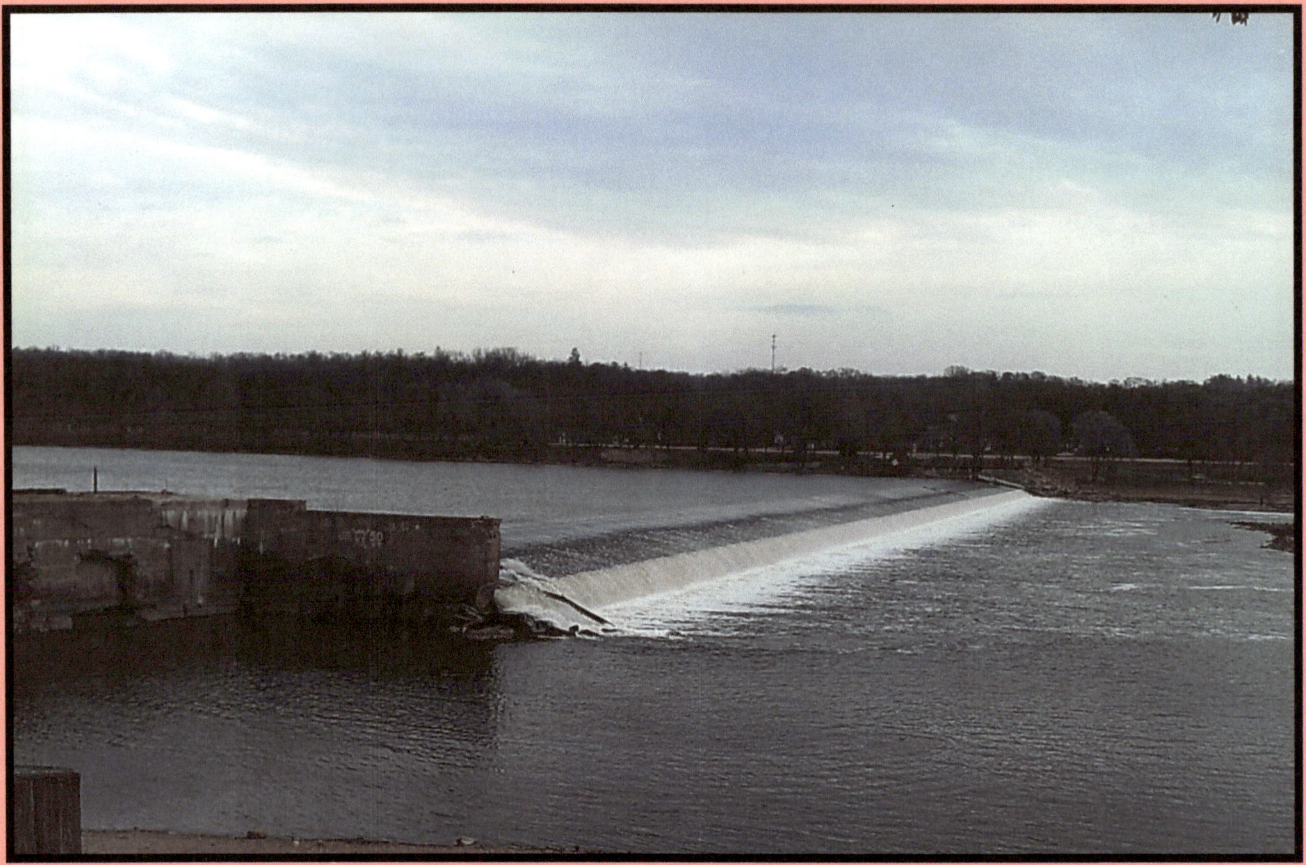

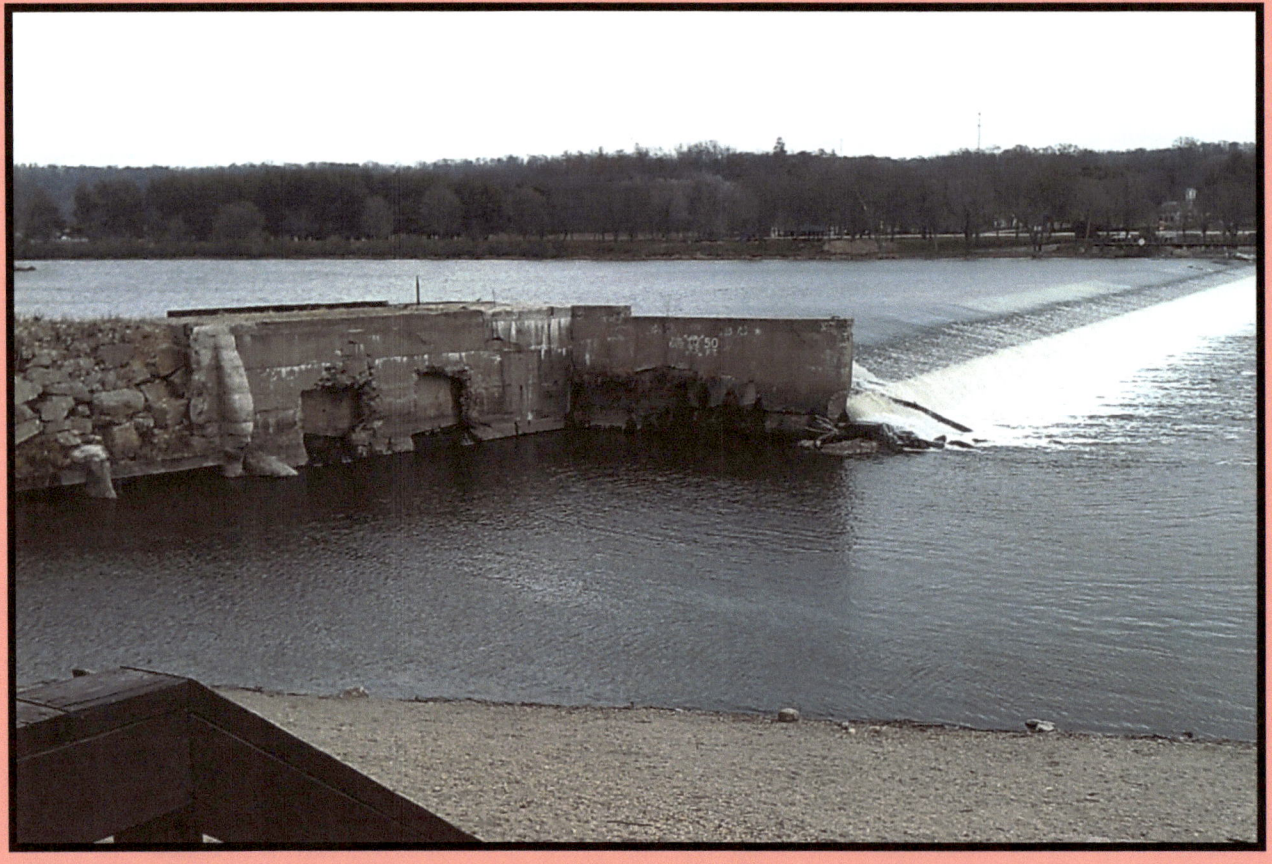

Hear the rush of the water...coolness in the day showed mostly in the sky...Outside
from behind HANOVER SQUARE Mall from OREGON, ILLINOIS

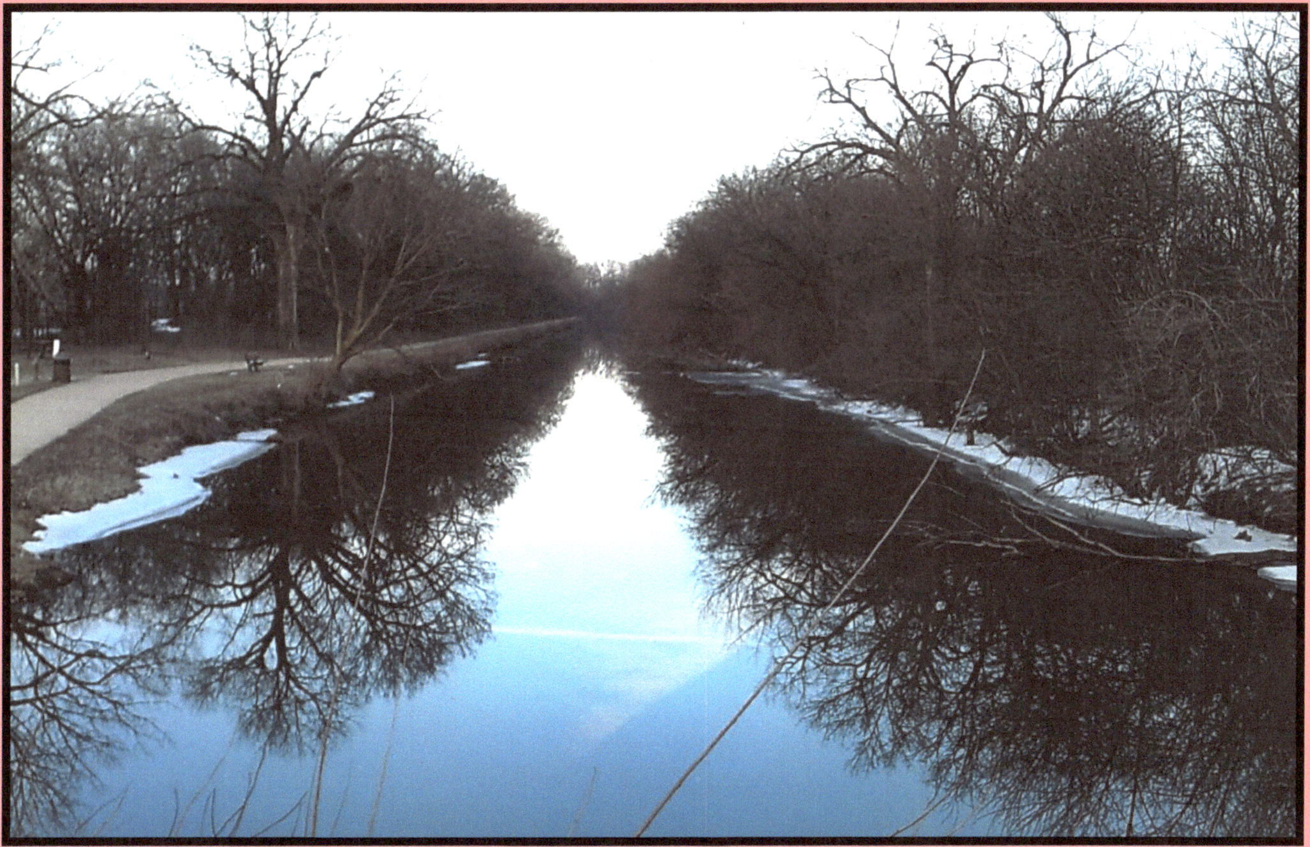

Wonder where that path went off to a head off of BUEL ROAD, this side goes to
ROCK FALLLS, ILLINOIS....

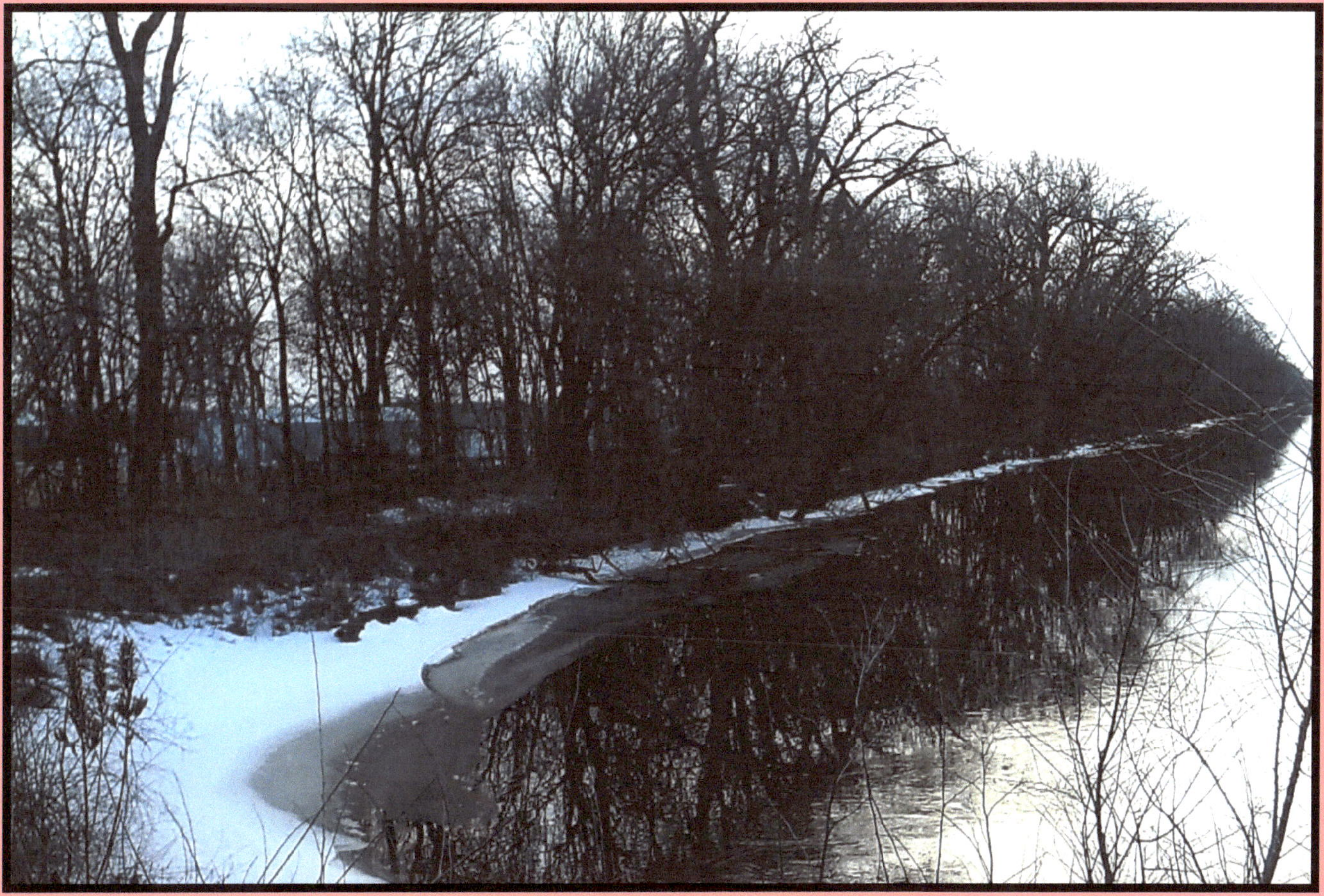

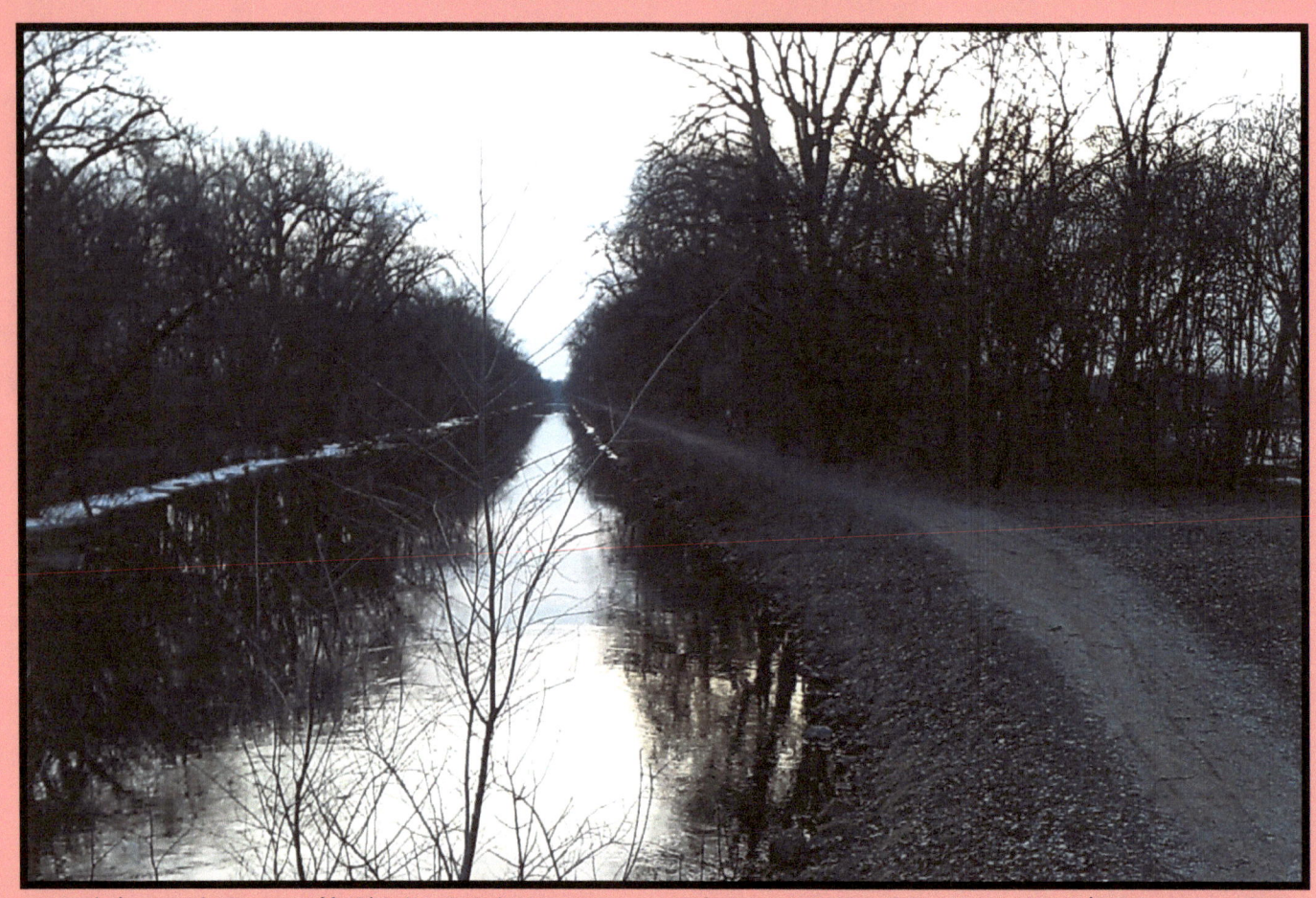

...this path ran off BUEL ROAD ran away from ROCK FALLLS, ILLINOIS towards a small town called PROPHERTS TOWN, ILLINOIS- Does it make it there? ....I wonder.

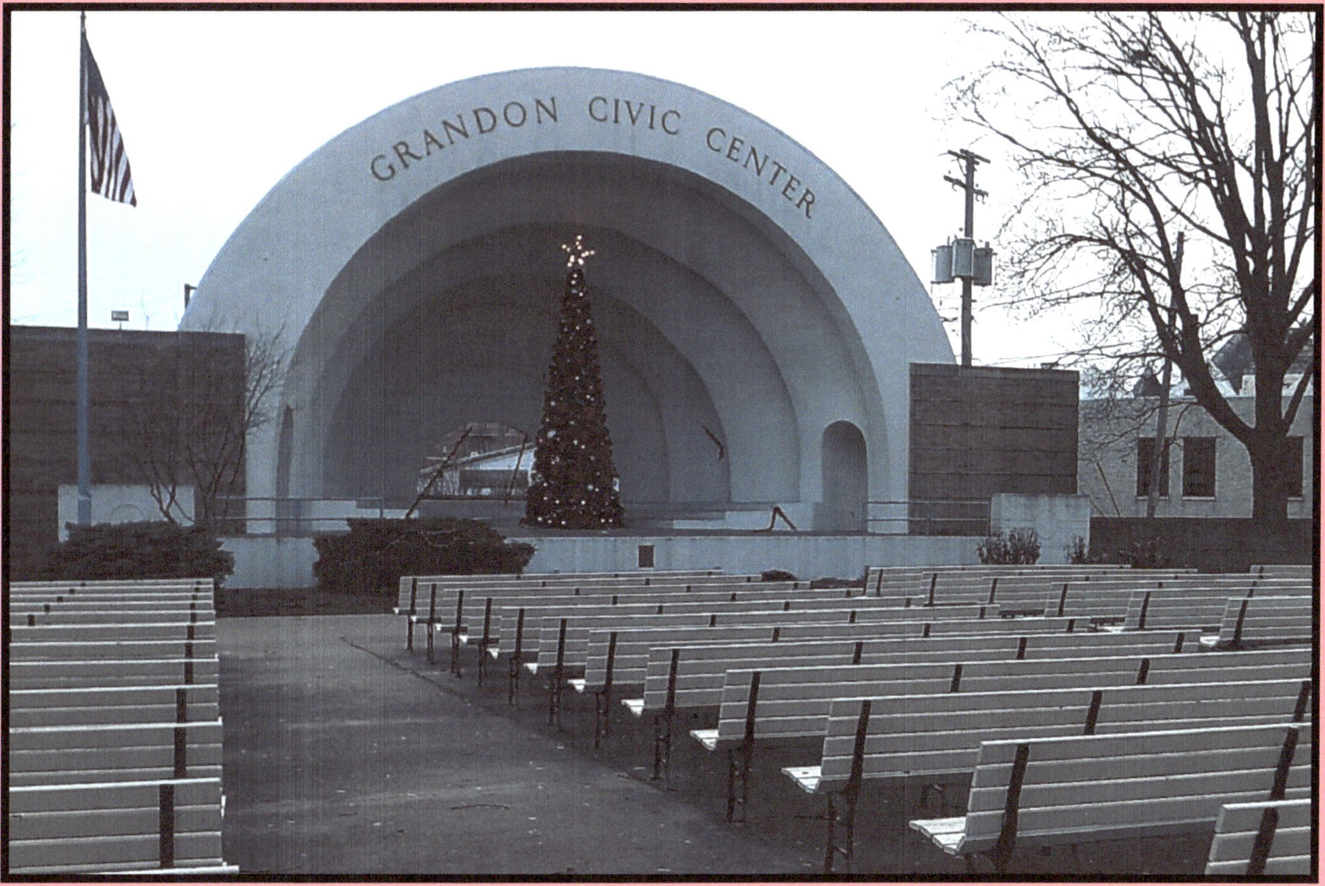

...Maybe the high school band or bride and groom will arrive on time...
STERLING, ILLINOIS...my holiday shown through with a thought or two...and

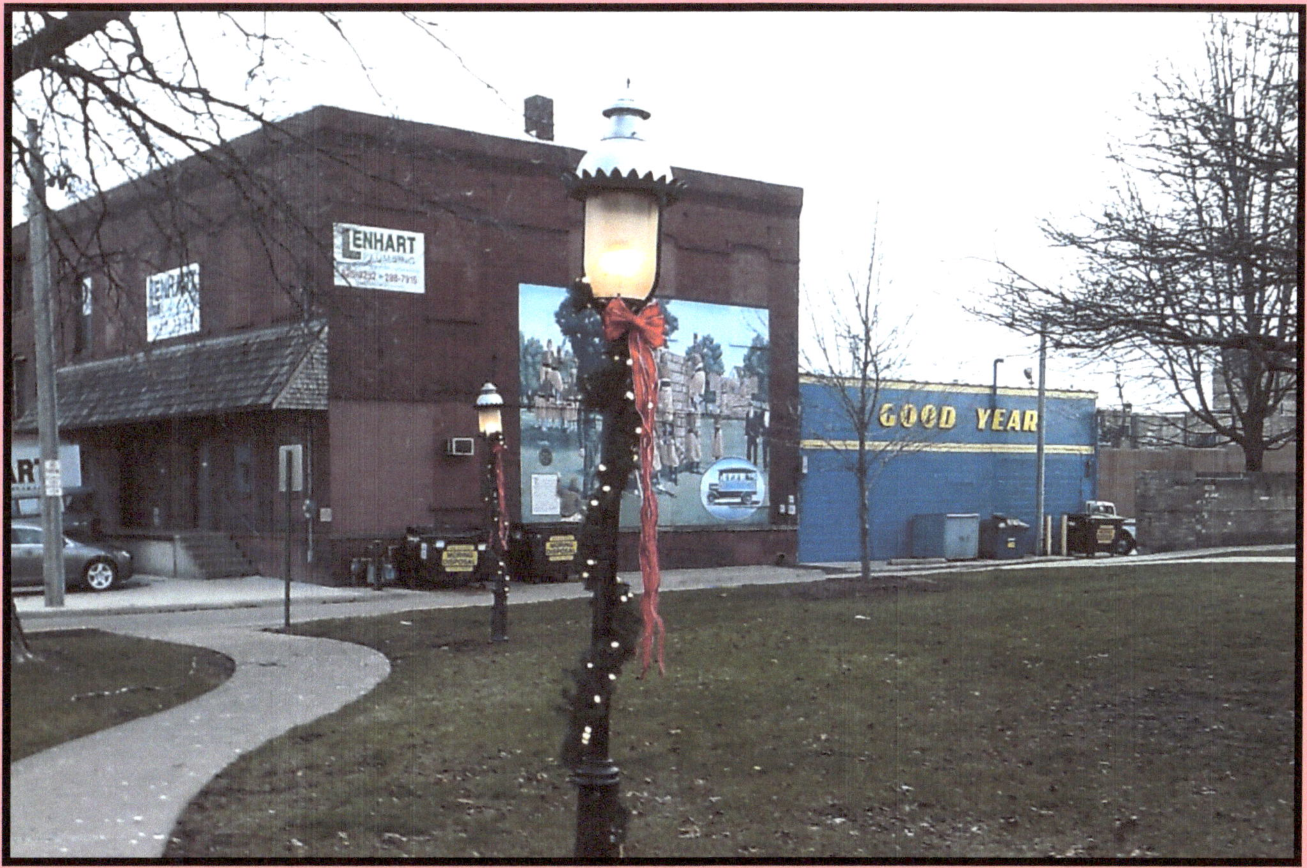

...there's a soldier always standing nearby in the same park...

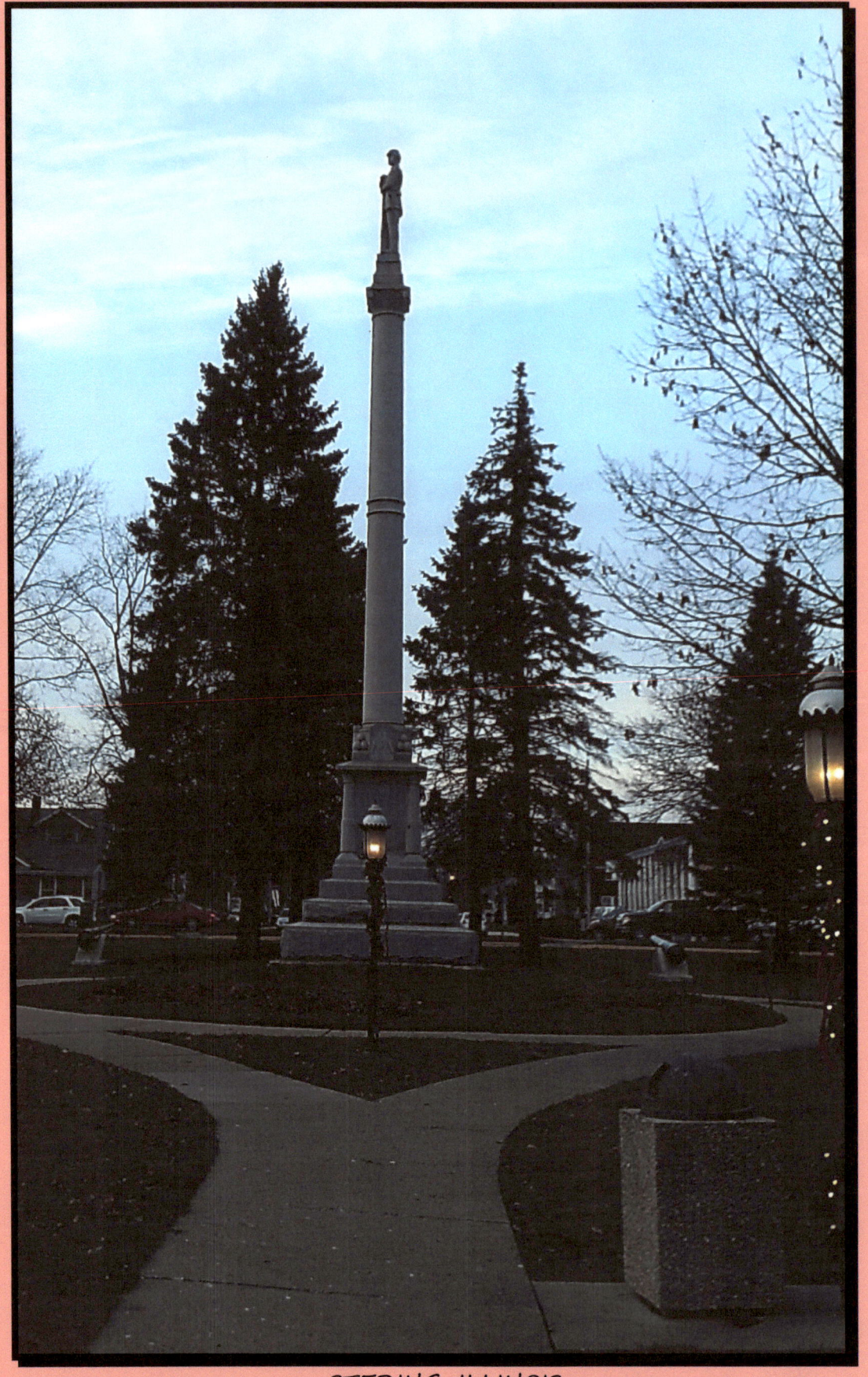

STERING, ILLINOIS

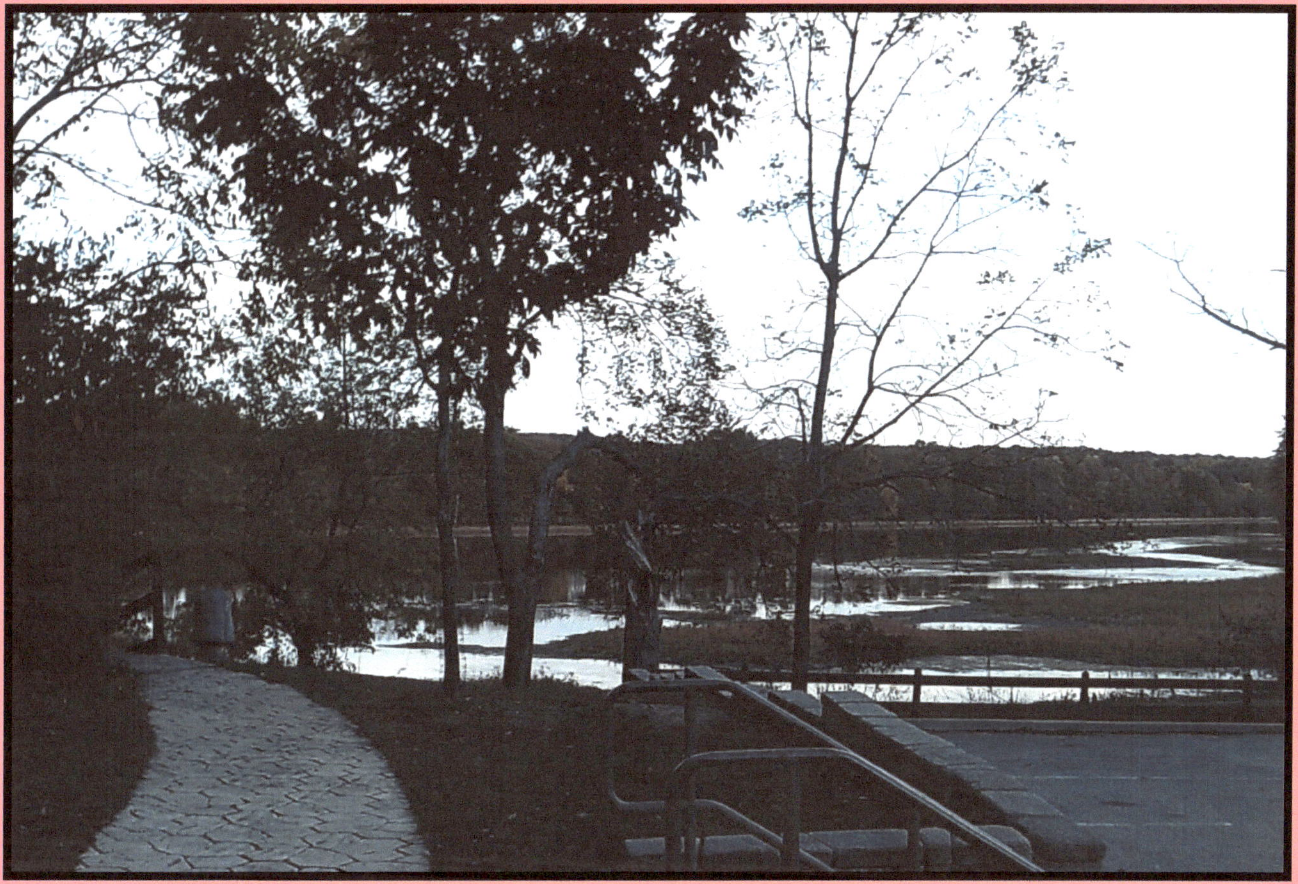

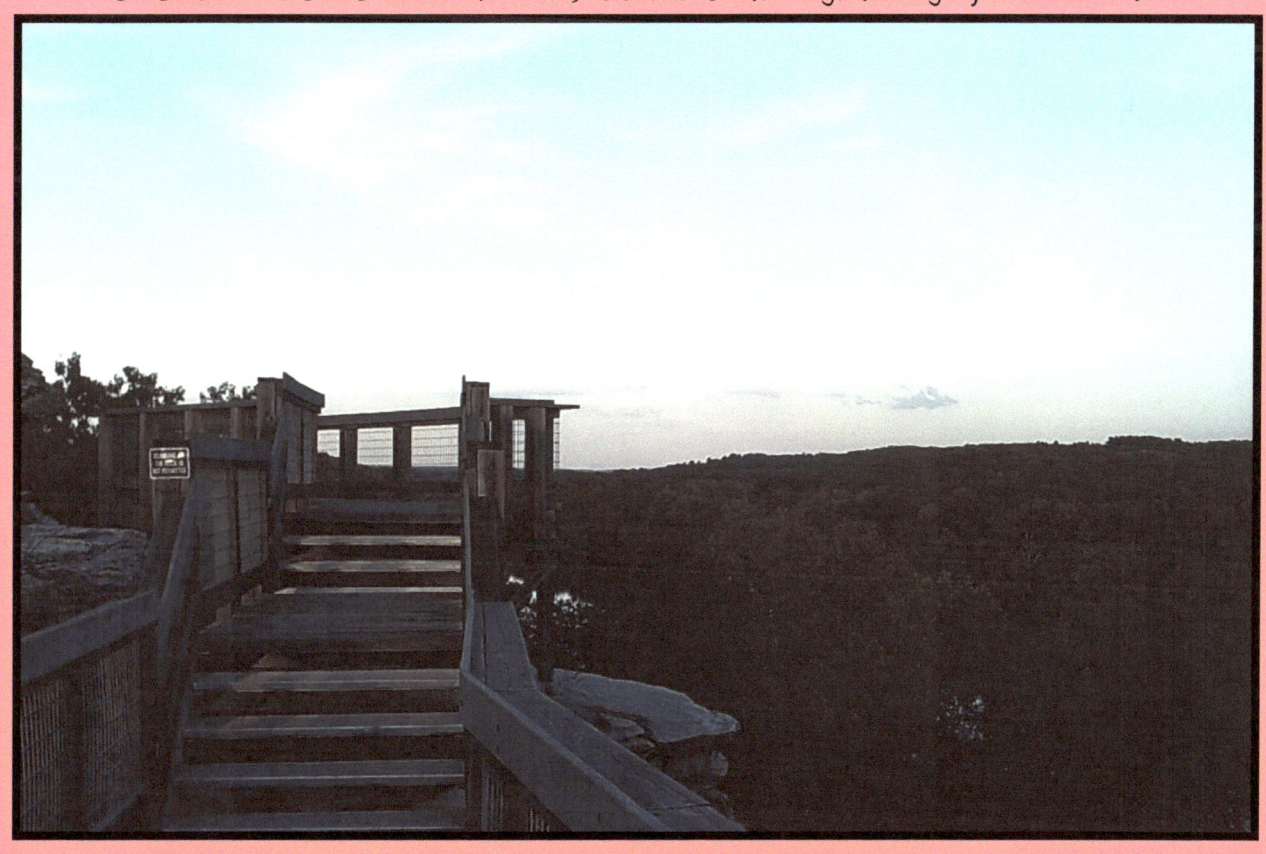

CASTLE ROCK STATE PARK, ILLINOIS...thought I'd go for a climb..

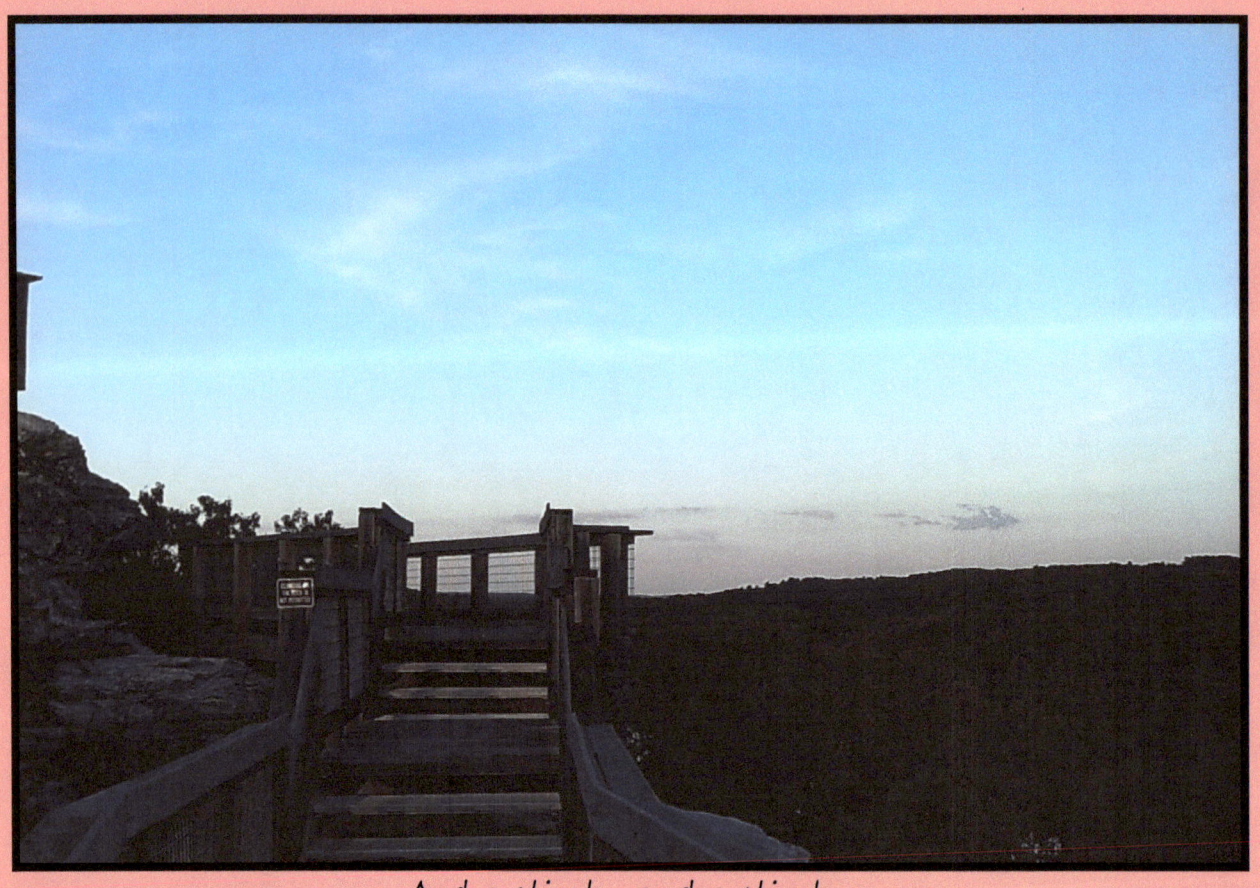

And a climb....and a climb...

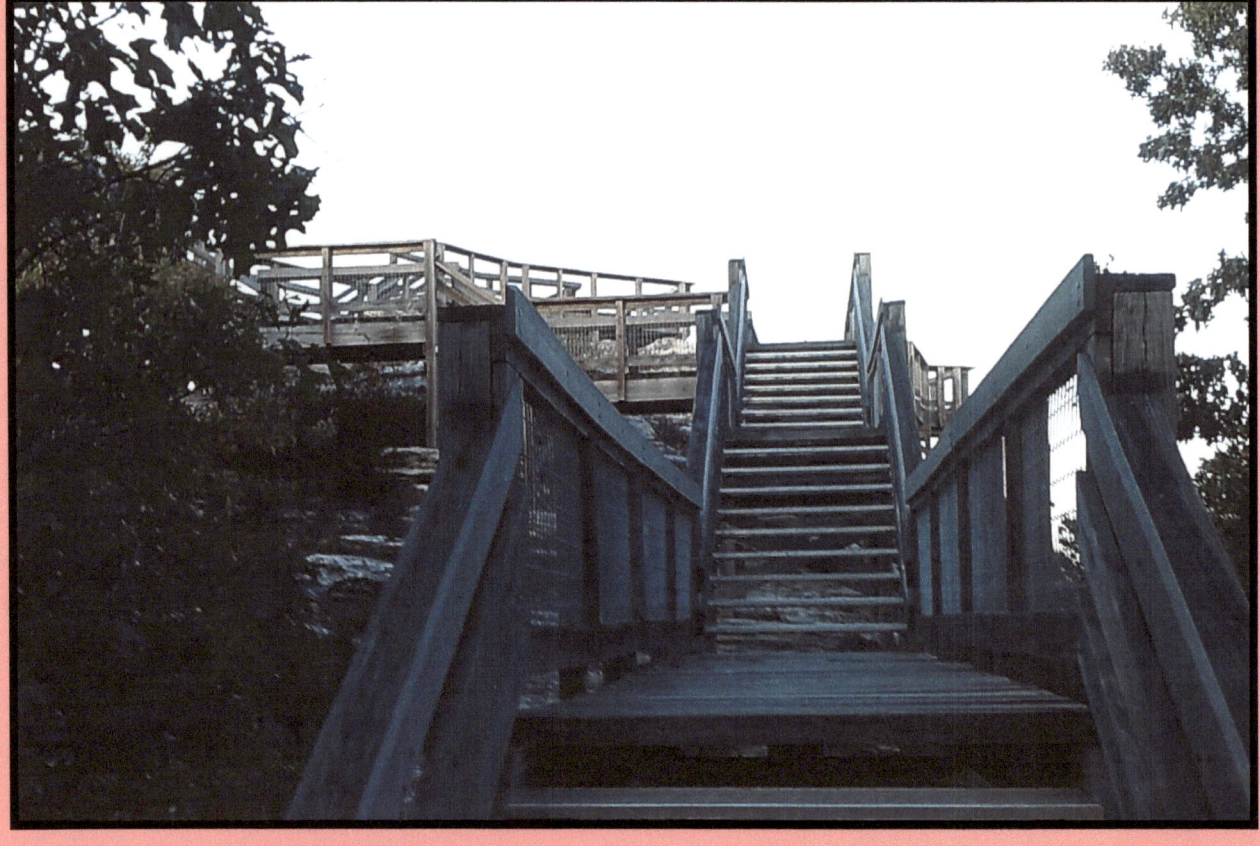

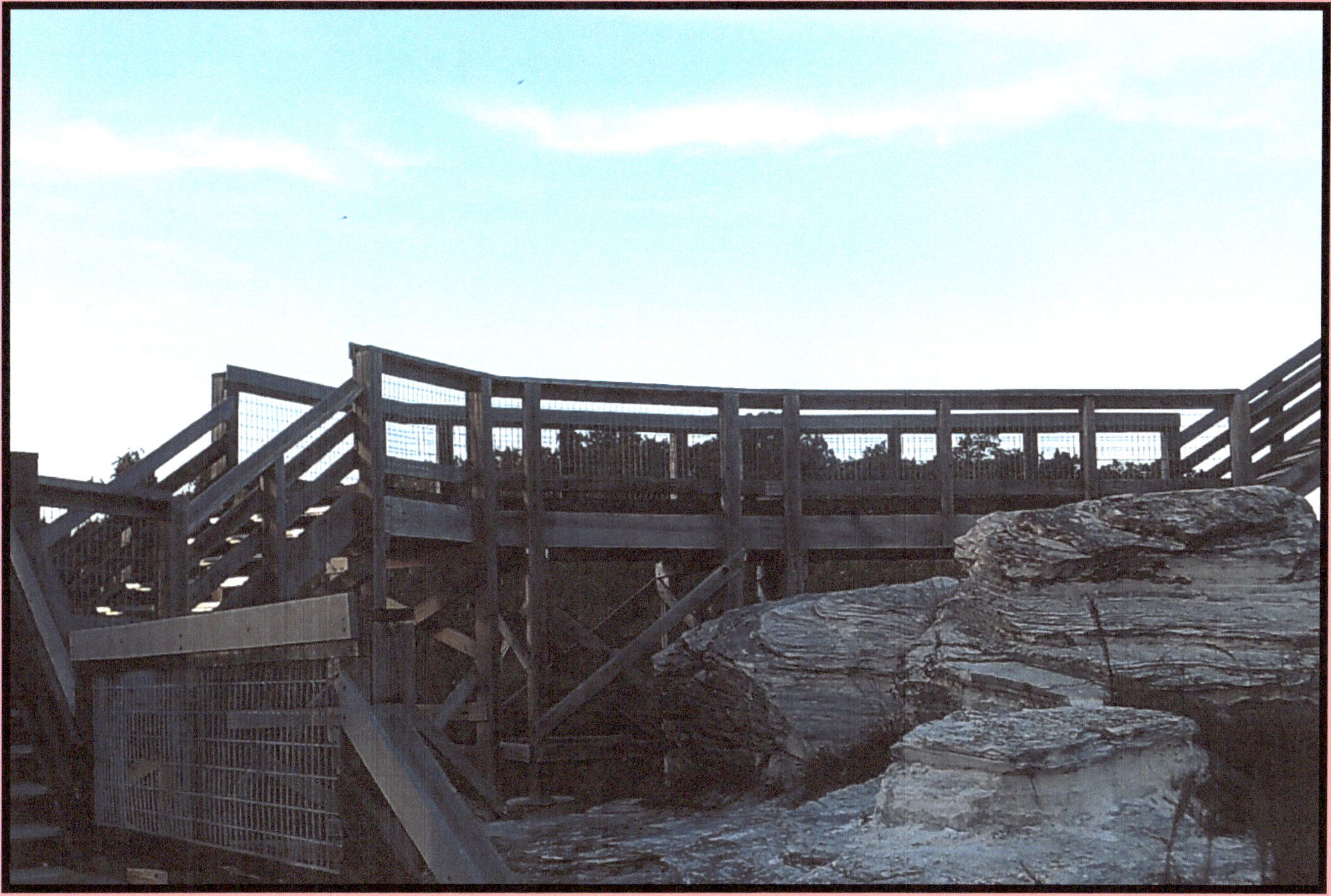

Oh! I reached the top!. Now for a descend ...

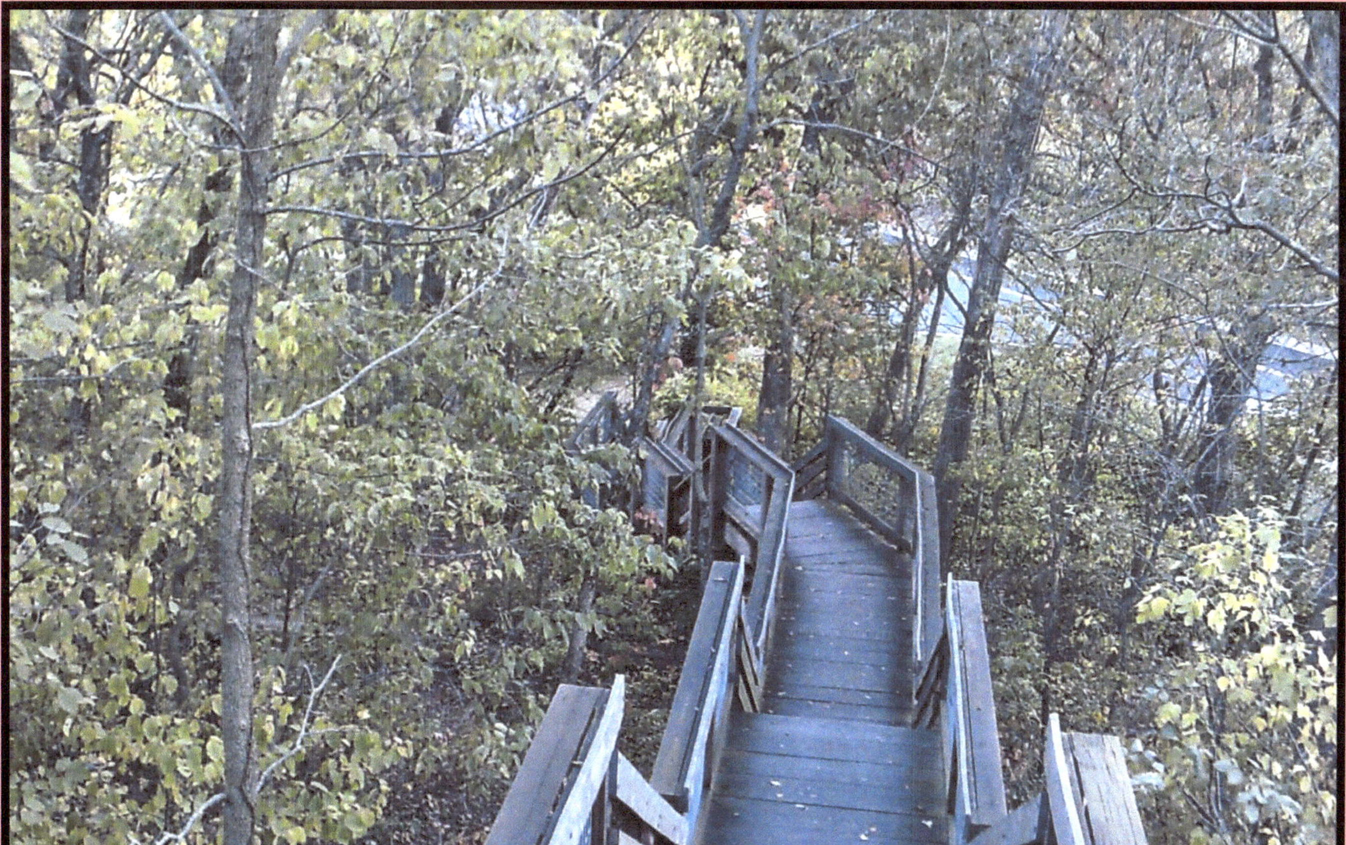

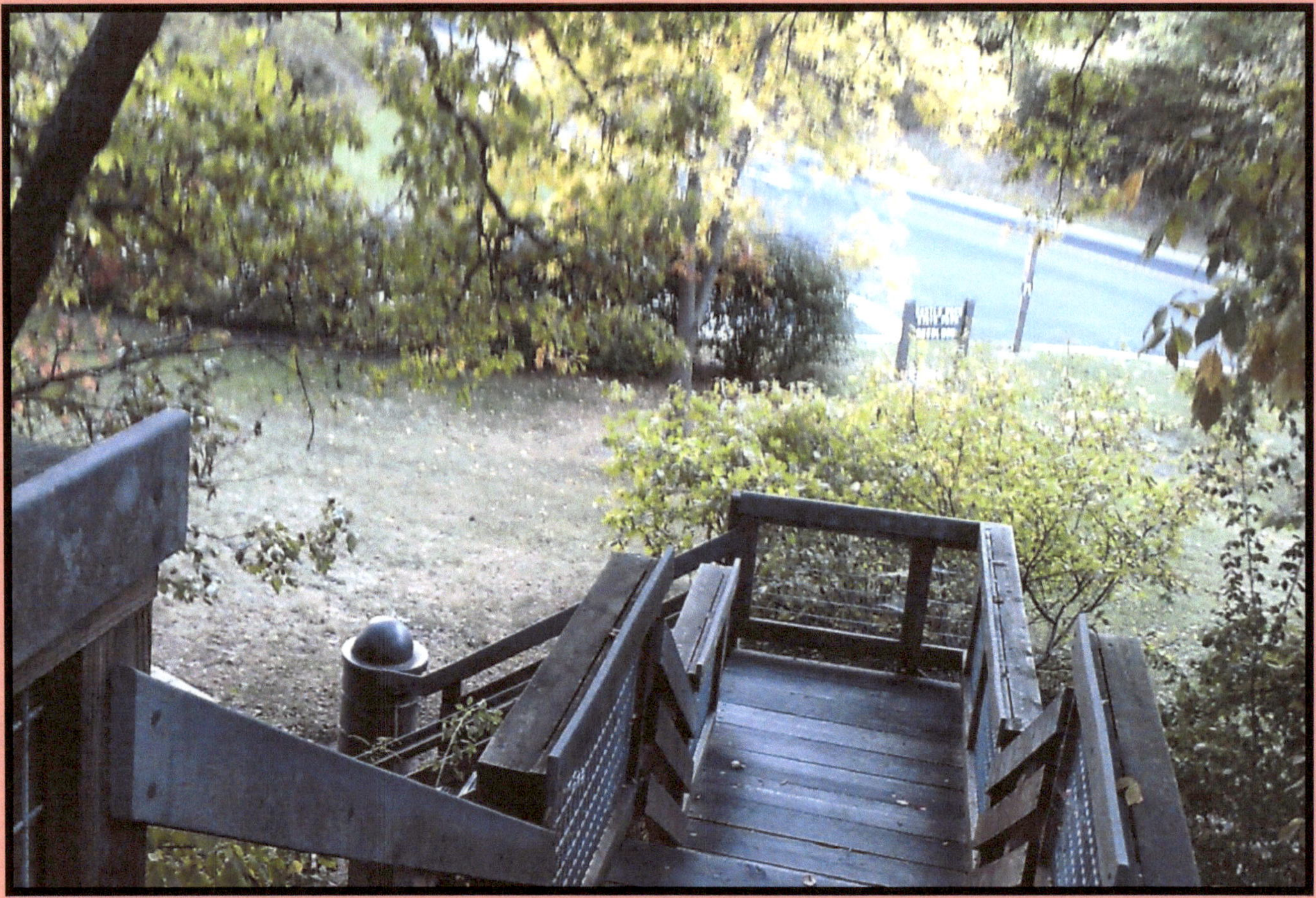

What a day at CASTLE ROCK STATE PARK, ILLINOIS with the Moon!

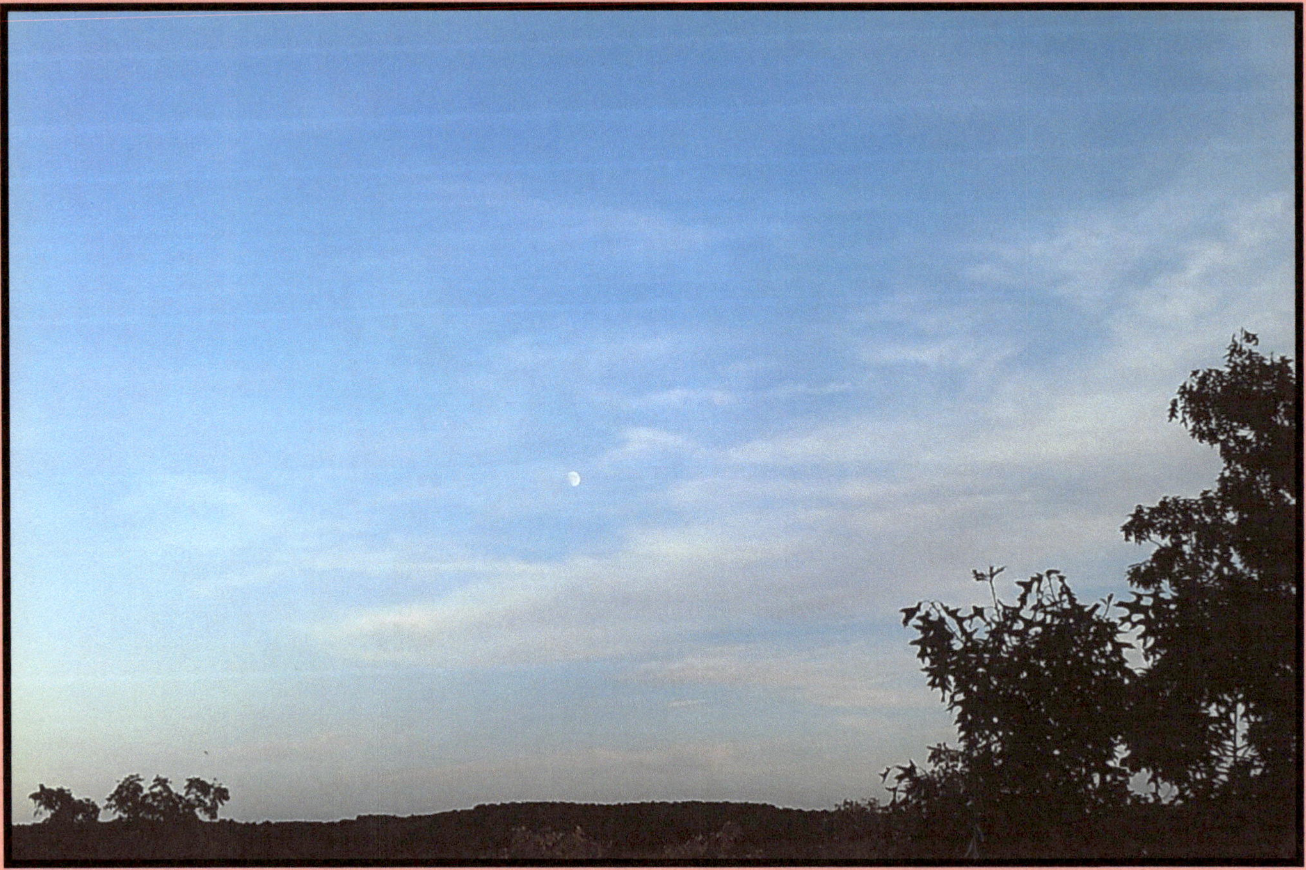

www.sightwordsataglance.com is an independent educator contractor website. The website is promotes free education for all ages for a hope for a better day after tomorrow. Proceeds of royalties from this book and the below products will go towards the independent educator contractor to continue work in hopes that a foundation will be formed with the name

www.sightwordsataglance.com

The website is currently circulated among the *United States Pentagon, United Nations* and *North Dakota Indian Reservations* along with a few *learning institutes.*

Thanks to those that purchase this product.

May life continue to be stronger throughout the world.

Other products offered on amazon.com from the same independent educator contractor are:
Additional **Books** available on amazon.com:

'My Native American Indian Boy' (Novel on Perception)
'My Dog Hiccup' (4th and 5th Grade Comprehension Readers)
'Orange's 9th Birthday' (4th and 5th Grade Comprehension Readers)
'Literary, Short Stories and Poetry' (Christian Content- Family Whole Some)
'Poetry' Family Poetry (Love, Family and Children)
'In My Philosophy and Understanding of God' Contains Human Interest Papers'

Book Series
Volume 1 'My Oregon Giant' (Introductory – The leave me alone stage of Life)
Volume 2 'My Oregon Giant Calming Adventure Christmas' (metaphorical thought)
Volume 3 'My Oregon Giant A Tale' (Christian content)

Book Series
Volume 1 'Mr. Alabaster Crane, Mister Gold Fish and Mr. Wood Pecker Goes to Grandma
            Alabaster Crane's Home' (Predators, circle of Life and Friendship)
Volume 2 'Mr. Alabaster Crane The Dilemma' Special Edition (New literature themed Civilization)

Work Booklets **(Illustrated definitions of words in a story)**
Volume 1 contains:
2 Sight Word Booklets, 'Mr. Squirrellie Makes Peanut Butter' and 'Who Plants the Flowers?'

Volume 2 contains:
3 Sight Word Booklets, 'Me and My Word', 'What Insect Am I?' and 'We make salad together from the backyard'

Games: Eye-Hand Motor Function
'Christmas Bingo Color Your Game Boards'
'Christmas Bingo Pig Color Your Game Boards'

www.ingramcontent.com/pod-product-compliance
Lightning Source LLC
Chambersburg PA
CBHW050430180526
45159CB00005B/2482